The NO-NONSENSE GUIDE to

WORLD FOOD

D1634302

'Humanity has lost its place within the biosphere as technology seems to give us mastery over the planet. But we remain profoundly biological beings as dependent on clean air, water, soil and energy and biodiversity as any other animal for our health and well being. The challenge of our time is to re-insert ourselves back into the natural world to recognize the complete unsustainability of the modern world.

'As globalization obscures locality of ecosystems and communities with brands and logos, the best way to recognize our true nature and needs is food. Every bit of our nutrition was once alive and we incorporate the fractured carcasses of plants and animals into our own bodies. What species do we consume, where, how and by whom were they reared and harvested, what was the ecological footprint of the food? Books like this get us started in our thinking and our actions.'

Dr David Suzuki

Science broadcaster, host of the globally syndicated
979.

700040767349

About the author
Wayne Roberts is a leading policy analyst and practitioner on how food intersects with public health and urban planning. Besides managing the Toronto Food Policy Council for many years, he has served on the Boards of the Community Food Security Coalition, Food Secure Canada, FoodShare and USC Canada. He speaks internationally on food policy councils and on ways to use food for successful cities. Follow him on Twitter @wrobertsfood.

Acknowledgements
This book comes out of an ecosystem or community of food practice. Aside from friends and supporters named in the text, I would like to thank Alison Blay-Palmer, Dana Stevof, Frank Van Bussel, Guido Van Rijkom, Leslie Toy, Michelle German-Macintosh and Walt Palmer for their support and ideas. My life partner, Lori Stahlbrand, is a top-notch food organizer and scholar in her own right, and helped me develop and refine most of the ideas in this book.

About the New Internationalist
New Internationalist is an independent, not-for-profit publishing co-operative that reports on issues of global justice. We publish informative current affairs and popular reference titles, complemented by multicultural recipe books, photography and fiction from the Global South, as well as calendars, diaries and cards – all with a global justice world view.

If you like this *No-Nonsense Guide* you will also enjoy the *New Internationalist* magazine. The magazine is packed full of high-quality writing and in-depth analysis, including:
- The Big Story: understanding the key global issues
- The Facts: accessible infographics
- Agenda: cutting-edge reports
- Country profile: essential insights and star ratings
- Argument: heated debate between experts
- Mixed Media: the best of global culture.
To find out more about the **New Internationalist**, visit our website at **newint.org**

The **NO-NONSENSE GUIDE** to

WORLD
FOOD

Wayne Roberts

New Internationalist

The No-Nonsense Guide to World Food
First published in the UK by
New Internationalist™ Publications Ltd
Oxford OX4 1BW, UK
First published 2008. This new edition 2013.
newint.org

© Wayne Roberts

The right of Wayne Roberts to be identified as the author of this work has been
asserted in accordance with Copyright, Designs and Patents Act 1998.

All rights reserved. No part of this book may be reproduced, stored in a
retrieval system or transmitted, in any form or by any means, electronic,
electrostatic, magnetic tape, mechanical, photocopying, recording or
otherwise, without prior permission in writing of the Publisher.

Series editor: Chris Brazier
Design by New Internationalist Publications Ltd.
Cover image: Melhi / Getty Images

Printed by T J International Limited, Cornwall, UK, who hold environmental
accreditation ISO 14001.

MIX
Paper from
responsible sources
FSC® C013056
www.fsc.org

British Library Cataloguing-in-Publication Data.
A catalogue record for this book is available from the British Library.

Library of Congress Cataloging-in-Publication Data.
A catalog for this book is available from the Library of Congress.

ISBN 978-1-78026-131-7

Foreword

A *No-Nonsense Guide to World Food* couldn't be more timely, especially given the great deal of rubbish being served to a public hungry for answers about their food. One of the common themes, which the food industry has been very keen to promote, is this: 'If we just choose the right things at the supermarket, all will be well.'

That's the kind of nonsense that this book has none of. After all, if the answer to the problem of our food is 'shopping', you've got to wonder what the question was. The surge of interest in food comes at a time when people around the world, particularly in poorer countries, are thinking about food with unprecedented sophistication, organization and creativity.

Take, for instance, the work of the Via Campesina international peasant movement. It's one of the world's largest social movements with, by some estimates, up to 100 million members, in rich and poor countries, comprised of the world's poorest farmers and landless workers. They have been at the wrong end of our collapsing industrial food supply for decades, and so they know better than most what works and what doesn't. They've come up with a new vision for a worldwide future for food. It's called 'food sovereignty'.

It's a vision with some fairly clear ideas about what needs to happen so that small farmers can survive, that the environment is maintained, and that there is global justice. But food sovereignty embodies perhaps the most important lesson from years of struggle around food and agriculture: the best way to arrive at a balanced, just, and sustainable food system is to have a democratic conversation about it. The power should be in all our hands and, too often, it feels like it isn't. One thing that makes the idea of food sovereignty daunting is the fact that we've never really had a democratic conversation about food. The way our food comes to us has been shaped by corporations and governments, international institutions and oligarchs. It doesn't feel like we have much to say in the bigger debate. And the number of questions that we might begin such a conversation with are, frankly, a little overwhelming: where should I shop?, what should I eat?, what can I do to help farmers overseas?, what's a food mile and should I care about them?, can the whole world really eat organic?, what are we going to do about eating in cities?

The book in your hands not only has the answers but, better yet, the questions to ask in a further, and richer, democratic debate about our food. It's a debate that Wayne Roberts' powerful book will prime you for. The conversation and the road ahead is not easy, but it's one whose rewards could not be sweeter.

Raj Patel

Author of *Stuffed and Starved: Markets, Power and the Hidden Battle for the World Food System*

CONTENTS

Introduction

EVENTS SINCE the first edition of this book came out in 2008 make an impressive statement about the ability of modestly funded citizen groups to affect the food agenda, as well as the power of well-financed governments and large corporations to push back.

Here are six food highlights that couldn't have been predicted five years ago.

1 The field that used to be called Food Policy has broken wide open. Churches, business groups, farm organizations and political parties have developed wide-ranging food policies and strategies. But the place where food policies and strategies are having their greatest impact is in cities. I wrote the first edition of this book when I was managing the Toronto Food Policy Council, a leader among the handful of food policy councils in the world at the time. Today, there are well over 200, and food is well on the road to being recognized as a pillar of city and regional planning. New York leads all governments in programs to limit aggressive marketing of products causing obesity. Belo Horizonte, Brazil, leads in anti-hunger initiatives. Havana, Cuba, leads in urban agriculture. London made the breakthrough on sustainable fish. Markham, in the Canadian province of Ontario, set the bar on government purchasing of local sustainable food. Small villages in India and Honduras confirm that farmers need to be partners in breeding resilient seeds for climate change.

2 Food grew up to become a youth movement. It really shows at universities, many of which serve fair trade drinks alongside local and sustainable meals. Food studies, an unheard of area until recently, has blossomed. Youth have put food all over the social media, and are embracing careers in artisanal food production, agriculture and advocacy.

3 Food prices shot up and stayed up. In 2008, desperately hungry people held stormy protests in about 40 countries. Some set the stage for the Arab Spring of 2010, a geopolitical shift of first-rate importance. Indeed, fear of food shortages became a geopolitical shift in its own right, the background to unregulated speculation in food stocks as well as to 'land grabs' of tens of millions of well-watered hectares of quality land throughout Africa. In 2010, failure to manage hunger events led food agencies of the United Nations to open their meetings to global citizen group participation. Countering that, in 2011, the wealthy G8 nations partnered with major global corporations to launch a more private club, the New Alliance for Nutrition and Food Security, to fund industrialization of African agriculture. The World Trade Organization, which brashly set out to push deregulated global food trade and investment during the 1990s, is fading from the scene, but its agenda is proceeding slowly and without publicity through regional trade pacts. For good or ill, food has moved to center stage in world politics.

4 The biofuels industry, which converts foodlands for people into fuel-lands for cars, has ramped up since 2008, reducing grains available for food. Rising meat production has the same impact. Both trends directly affect hunger, health, community development and the environment – showing how many vital global questions hinge on food supplies.

5 Positive change is 'scaling up'. Fair trade sales continue to soar. Organic sales hit $60 billion in 2010, rising steadily in the Global North, and most rapidly in Brazil and China. Walmart is the big player in organics. In 2010, Unilever, a giant of processed foods, made a commitment to source all farmed products sustainably by 2020. Change is happening in big-time food markets.

6 We learned from Brazil and Cuba that both hunger and desperate poverty can be overcome. The central place of government policies, largely a missing link in the changes sweeping the world, is confirmed.

Food is at the forefront of transformative changes that will be outlined in this new edition of *The No-Nonsense Guide to World Food*. The rise of food as a complex of issues requires change at every level – from the individual through the whole of society to government.

The next six chapters will outline the conceptual tools to understand why food is coming to the forefront in many transformational ways. In Chapter 1, I introduce the concept of food systems and explain why a systems analysis is fundamentally important. Chapter 2 provides the history and context for the current industrial food system. Chapter 3 explains why a system that produces cheap food ends up exacerbating hunger and environmental degradation. Chapter 4 introduces the concept of 'food sovereignty' as the counter to an industrial food system. Chapter 5 discusses why hunger is still a pressing issue globally, and explains what two countries – Brazil and Cuba – have done about it. Finally, Chapter 6 looks to the future and presents seeds of hope coming from the global food movement.

I hope this new edition helps people understand and engage with these momentous opportunities. Enjoy!

Wayne Roberts
Toronto

1 Introducing the food system

The concept of a 'food system' helps explain many of the problems and opportunities in today's confusing and fast-changing global food scene. Food systems are sometimes described as 'hidden in plain sight' – only obvious after they've been pointed out. The same goes for food's healing powers, which can be tapped by people looking to make a difference in their lives, careers and communities.

FOOD IS a hot topic these days, for two totally different reasons. First, many people realize that food as they've known it can no longer be taken for granted. They're unsure how to protect themselves from unsettling trends in food safety and food processing, the rapid rise of obesity and chronic disease, or levels of poverty that impose hunger and malnutrition. Second, and in a totally different vein, many people are excited about heartwarming food projects that help them find their voice and satisfy their desires for a meaningful, engaged, empowered and authentic life. The world of food is poised on the edge of problems and opportunities. Welcome to a subject that impacts upon everyone, and invites everyone to make a difference.

At issue is a New Food Equation. It's not your grandmother's food equation. The industrial formula that took enormous strides toward delivering ample, affordable, healthy and safe food in the Global North during the 1950s and 1960s hasn't lived up to its reputation in the Global North, and isn't making much positive headway in the Global South. The anticipations of an earlier generation are being disappointed just as a new generation emerges with rising aspirations – that food should taste real, provide fulfilling careers, support health, contribute to local communities, honor the environment, and enhance global sustainability. X marks the spot where dashed expectations meet rising ones, creating what Welsh academic Kevin Morgan calls the New Food Equation.[1]

The 'food problem' problem

There are two general ways of responding to the New Food Equation. The standard way is to present the challenge as a 'food problem', and to urge people to solve the problem by making good food choices rather than bad ones. One column on a typical chart could have a heading for good foods, and the other column could have a heading for bad foods. The two-way split of foods would carry on down the columns – healthy foods versus junk foods; vegetarian meals rather than heavy servings of meat; low-fat against high-fat; organic in place of conventional; local as opposed to imported; cooked from scratch as an alternative to highly processed; slow versus fast, and so on.

The premise of this standard view is that there's a 'food problem', or at least a problem with specific foods. This approach makes common sense for many people because it corresponds to everyday food experiences that either feel good or bad. The approach also fits with popular beliefs that individuals need to make responsible choices about what foods to avoid and which ones to eat. In my experience, this 'food problem' approach is largely unquestioned – almost a given. When I'm invited to give a talk about food outside of my hometown, for example, local journalists almost always start by asking what food problems I'll discuss. Will I talk about the food problem of the world's 1.8 billion people who eat too much for their own good, or the food problem of the billion people who eat too little, or the food waste problem?

This line of questioning leaves me tongue-tied because I don't like to talk about food when it falls under the shadow of the word 'problem'. I want to shift the discussion to what I would call governance or system problems. To paraphrase former US President

Bill Clinton, I believe there is nothing wrong with food that cannot be fixed by what is right with food. For example, it's not a food problem that leads to hunger. In 2005, enough food was produced to share a very filling 2,772 calories with every person in the world every day. In sub-Saharan Africa, where 27.6 per cent of people suffered from hunger, there was enough to provide everyone with 2,238 calories a day. South Asia, where 21.8 per cent of people are hungry, had enough for all to enjoy 2,293 calories a day. It's not a food problem that causes hunger. It's a system problem of people who can't manage abundance.[2]

The central argument of this first chapter is that blaming food problems and bad food choices is a bad habit that needs to be broken. I like to trash junk food as much as the next person, but setting up a category for junk food gets us off on the wrong foot by underestimating the real proportions of the problem. Junk food needs to be seen along a spectrum, not as a separate category on the fringe. It's not a simple matter of poking fingers at the junk-food outlet over there. A good many mainstream foods have lost their original nutrients, are laden with salt, sugar, fat and empty calories, are prepared with minimal skills and eaten with little grace – not much difference from junk food there. For example, a popular case has been made that most grain for white, brown, whole-wheat and multi-grain bread, bagels and pasta has grown from seeds selected for baking and storage properties, not for nutritional quality, and has been stripped of wholesome fiber, and mixed with lavish amounts of salt, sugar and other additives. The same can be said for breakfast cereals.[3] Orange juice has gone down the same track: drinks companies own the dominant brands, and process the oranges in ways that remove most of the original goodness, a detailed study shows.[4] Likewise, another study points out that most Florida-grown tomatoes have been raised to sacrifice nutrients and taste for bright color (the credit for which goes to ethylene gas, not time out in the sun) and low price.[5] Prepared soups, sauces, salad dressings and sandwich spreads use ingredients and processing methods similar to junk-food outlets. People may go to a full-service restaurant or supermarket thinking they are choosing real food over junk food, but the ingredient list shows otherwise. If this is indeed a 'food problem', it's a bigger mess than just junk food.

The 'food problem' approach can mistakenly badmouth certain foods. Such mistakes remind me of a friend who survived a stroke but was frustrated by his inability to move his right arm, which he called his 'bad arm'. Don't blame the arm, his physiotherapist told him; the problem is in your brain's message center. That principle applies to a wide range of 'bad foods' – coffee, tea, chocolate, sugar and salt among them – which have had their good side bent out of shape by a faulty control system. The bad reputation may be a result of too much of a good thing, or too much messing with a good thing.

A good example of this is palm oil, the second most traded edible oil in the world, found in about 10 per cent of processed foods, cosmetics and soaps (most famously Palmolive). Like so many other ingredients shipped around the world – check how many times you find palm oil, carrageen or guar gum on a food label, for instance – palm oil is used to stop combinations of food in prepared meals from losing shape, breaking apart or collapsing into themselves as sticky goo over a long life on the shelf. Palm oil is stable and solid at room temperature, and performs well under high heat. These qualities explain why it is widely used in baked and fried foods, make-believe creamers, whipped toppings, candies and cookies that spend a long time on shelves, and why the combo of chocolate and palm melts in your mouth, not your hands. But food critics smear it for its high saturated fat content, while environmentalists slam plantation-style palm monoculture for displacing millions of hectares of rainforest. Since almost all commercial palm oil comes from Malaysia and Indonesia, it accounts for a good portion of the mileage that processed foods cover as they travel from farm to fork.

Who would ever guess that the palm oil squeezed by hand from the pulped fruit of the original palm tree of western Africa is something of a wonderfood, high in Vitamins E, K, A and 'good' cholesterol? In its home base in Africa, the multi-purpose palm tree was raised as one of several trees in a forest garden, and offered up its leaves for disposable wrappers around meats, cattle feed, basket weaving and thatched roofs, while its sap was used to make a relatively nutritious sweetener and delicate wine. 'Like so many African treasures,' investigative reporter Joan Baxter writes, 'once the foreign industrialists got their hands on it and took it away, the oil palm became something quite different' – its fruit processed beyond recognition. But that's not a food problem or a palm-tree problem. Making it seem that way just serves to deflect attention from the real problem of an inadequate food governance system.[6]

The need to shift focus from food problems to food systems is confirmed by an overview of giant food companies. A 2010 survey of the world's top 50 food companies showed that 49 of them sold mostly highly processed, highly refined, high-fat, high-salt, highly packaged, highly advertised, high-calorie, low-nutrient foods, snacks, soda pops and alcohol. Dole, known for marketing fruit, stands out as a top company that sells stand-alone foods. The success of the top 50 indicates that consumers around the world are eating up the items found on food problem lists. Israel, Qatar and Oman are among a handful of countries where people spend more money on fruit and vegetables than on booze and tobacco.[7] This 2010 survey, which has been largely ignored in the media, raises some interesting questions. First, why does hardly anyone recognize the names of more than 10 of the world's top 50 food syndicates? 'Food problems' are often linked to highly advertised and well-known junk-food chains, not to gray and greasy eminences. Something more systemic than famous companies and products must be at work. Discovering that force leads away from a simple chart of food problems towards analysis of food systems.

The way governments approach food also sheds light on the need to think beyond a list of food problems. Chew on the Canada Food and Drug Act definition of food: 'any article manufactured, sold or represented for use as food or drink for human beings, chewing gum, and any ingredient that may be mixed with food for any purpose whatever'. No problem figuring out how the prefabricated Tim Hortons donut became Canada's national food, though how this wording gets repeated virtually word for word in US and European law bears inquiry into either plagiarism or the power of the chewing gum lobby. The law makes no reference to food being grown, foraged, cultivated, nurtured or raised, and only specifies food as being manufactured, which speaks to the industrial mindset of the post-1940s world when the modern food system developed. The law gives blanket authorization to companies to describe any manufactured good they produce as food. In one fell swoop, this pulls the rug out from under public health advocates, who often refer to high-fat/high-sugar/high-salt foods as 'competitive' foods, because they compete for customer loyalty and stomach space with healthy foods that don't have an advertising budget. Under the law, competitive foods enjoy all the tax-free, subsidy and regulatory advantages that healthy foods enjoy, and none of the tax and regulatory costs of presenting themselves for what they really are – risky amusement or entertainment products with little resemblance to anything that passed for food before 1940. When governments embed this approach to food in bedrock legislation, something is going on that goes beyond 'food problems', which wouldn't exist if the government didn't call them food.

A joyful approach to food

The 'food problem' discourse creates unnecessary anxieties and divisions among people who could be saving their energy for something positive. In 1931, Irma Rombauer wrote one of the best-selling cookbooks of all time, *The Joy of Cooking*. The book is a milestone because she defied all the messaging from food processors who depicted food preparation as drudgery akin to slavery. *The Joy of Cooking*, as subversive in her day as *The Joy of Sex* was 30 years later, came out and said the Joy word, right beside Cooking. Weirdly, the cooking hang-up has stuck around longer in some societies than the sex hang-up. The concept of food problems is its legacy. In 1995, I learned the joyful approach from Herb Barbolet, a pioneer of Canada's food movement. 'The biggest food problem is the failure to recognize food opportunities,' he told me at his Farm Folk City Folk office in Vancouver. I've been hooked on food ever since, as a way to get people engaged in doable projects that help them act on food and people opportunities. I like to present potential food projects, rather than advocate for them, as if I'm presenting a dessert tray, and let people pick a project that suits their tastes. Good meals have appetizers and treats, and food organizers can learn from that example.

Here's a typical suggestion I offer up on a platter. It doesn't sound too appetizing, but it whets the appetite for thinking outside the box of food problems and throws open the windows to food system strategies. Start with a typical people-caused food problem begging for a solution – two billion tons of food tossed onto the garbage heaps of the world every year – well over a third of the food that's produced.[8] The beginning of wisdom here is to recognize that waste is a verb, not a noun. Nature has no toxic waste dumps or landfills.

Introducing the food system

Waste not , want not?

This chart shows that food waste is created primarily within the food suppy chain, not, as media stories commonly suggest, at the consumer end. In Europe and North America, average per person waste averages 280-300 kilograms a year. In sub-Saharan Africa and South Asia, per person waste averages 6-11 kilograms a year.

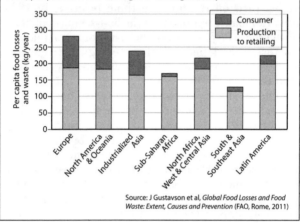

Source: J Gustavson et al, *Global Food Losses and Food Waste: Extent, Causes and Prevention* (FAO, Rome, 2011)

Only human civilizations create those. Wasting is an action that actually costs money – check the cost of pick-up, hauling, land-filling and landfill maintenance to any local government. By contrast, converting rotting food to high-end compost or biofuel, and then selling the finished products, is a money-maker and job creator for any city. Likewise, it costs more to haul stale but safe food to a dump than to provide it for livestock, another way to make both food and money instead of wasting food and money. Unsolvable problems are just brilliant disguises for great opportunities, US President Eisenhower used to say in the can-do 1950s. From this perspective, people who classify food as a problem have got the chain of causation backward. Food is the solution, a cause for joy and positive energy, not a problem, a source of anxiety and conflict.

Behind the failure to deal with food waste is a system error. The system error comes from deeply buried assumptions of which many officials are unaware. The food system keeps people from seeing or responding to waste because agriculture is modeled on extractive resource industries, which take an inert mineral from one area and turn it into a product sold in another area, where it eventually breaks down and is dumped in yet another area – a linear or assembly-line model. In industry-based trade publications, food is commonly referred to as an FMCG, or Fast-Moving Consumer Good – a disposable product like any other. Words used to describe food businesses – food industry, food production, packaged goods industry, food processing and so on – deny the biological nature of food and overlook the web of life linking humans and food and food and the environment. That leads to a 'waste management system' based on disposal of dead waste products, rather than a resource management system based on maintaining the circle of life. This is not a food problem or a food waste problem, but a system problem, embedded deep in the unconscious of individuals and entire economies. The problem has been 'invisibilized', but can be deftly managed with a little forethought when it's out in the open.

Using food as a tool

Talking about systems scares some people off because they think that leads to a nightmare of analysis-paralysis, where everything is connected to everything else and nothing practical can ever be disconnected and put in a bucket list. My experience as a manager and promoter of food policy for Toronto shows the opposite. In the food sector at least, success comes from finding a problem that can be fixed – or rather, an opportunity that can be tapped – by leveraging unused capacity, or what Dutch ecologist Gaston Remmers calls 'dormant capital' that was hidden in plain sight because of 'system blindness'. System blindness is akin to fridge blindness, common among people who can't find a bottle of milk in the middle of the fridge because their preoccupied mind overlooks the obvious. System blindness in a food context is due to bureaucrats not seeing that a problem can be fixed by using food as a tool.

In a typical scenario, a systems-minded designer of food programs is looking for a champion to do the work of plucking what is called low-hanging fruit. A dogged and focused but socially skilled and credible champion is the unsung hero and indispensable ingredient of any food policy recipe, because it is his/her job to cajole officials into acting outside their comfort level and job description, and to beg employers for forgiveness, not ask for permission. Champions are the mechanics of food system change, and epitomize the Power of One to make a difference. They can make the sustainable attainable.

To give credit where it's due, food is well adapted to creative problem-solving because it often presents as low-hanging fruit – an easy problem that can be solved while saving or making money. A whole category of food solutions is associated with unused capacity or dormant capital – the most plentiful resources in the world. An empty flat roof, a vacant lot, a bin full of food scraps, rain going down a sewer, hot water going down the drain after doing the dishes, a stove and sink in a church basement, are all examples of dormant capital. Unused capacity usually has two features. First, it has already been paid for. The landlord has already paid for a strong roof, and the homeowner has already paid for the hot water used to wash dishes. Second, it costs more to waste the asset than use it. This is most obvious with food scraps treated as garbage, which is very expensive to manage. It doesn't take too much chutzpah to ask that the unused capacity be donated free to a food cause, and that a fee be paid for a good portion of the cost avoided when a food organization uses the asset. This allows the food cause to benefit from two revenue streams – one for solving a problem, and a later one for providing a new opportunity. This is the secret of legendary greenhouse gardener Will Allen, from Milwaukee in the US. He charges beer companies to dump their spent grain in his facility, and then he sells the compost made from the grain, after using the heat generated in the composting process to heat his greenhouses through the winter. He won and deserved a MacArthur Genius Award for thinking like that.

How might this work in a town or city? With re-imagination and championing, the flat roof can be converted to a roof garden using soil enriched with compost from food scraps. The garden will be watered by rain that otherwise spills off a cement roof into a sewage system, and thereby saves the city the cost of expanding sewers to handle the extra stress of sewage flash floods caused by intense rainfall in the era of global warming. City engineers appreciate the savings from avoiding an expensive overhaul of the sewage system, and donate some of their savings to the gardeners, who hire the at-risk youth hanging out on the vacant lot to start a community garden there. The youth gain both general employment-readiness skills and specific skills as gardeners and landscapers, and make a fresh start. The soil is enriched by composted food scraps from the neighborhood. As the neighborhood delights in the community garden, one homeowner, who happens to be a plumber, builds a backyard greenhouse that will use the heat from his discarded dishwashing water to heat the greenhouse during the winter, and use the nutrient-rich water itself for irrigation. The backyard greenhouse and community garden produce enough surplus food to make a donation to the neighborhood church, which uses its previously unused basement kitchen equipment to sponsor a community kitchen for neighbors working on their cooking skills.

Were these really food problems that had to be overcome? I don't think so. Any losers in the new scenario? I doubt it. In fact, such changes usually lead to quadruple wins – one each for the environment, health, community, and government treasury. Opportunities come from working with food as a many-splendored asset that needs to be unlocked from the government department of agriculture that sees food just as a commodity to be sold rather than for its wider value as a community animator.

What is system thinking?

To better understand food in the context of a system – either in a small neighborhood, or around the world – try three exercises.

First, think of the earth as part of a solar system. Many things that happen on earth come from being part of a solar system. People don't often see it that way because the planet seems to be a self-contained stand-alone operation. That's why very smart people still talk about sunrise and sunset, when it's really the earth spinning around the sun. Day and night, summer and winter, tides, moonlight, being held in place by gravity – all these all-important but seemingly unrelated realities can only be understood on a system level. Or think of the parallel with the body's circulatory system or endocrine system. Ear, nose and throat is a combined medical specialty because each part is distinct but also functions in an integrated way, so parts need to be examined and treated in relationship to a whole.

For your next system exercise, think of arranging all yellow blocks on one side of a Rubik's Cube. It can't be done, unless you synch each move to what happens on all six sides of the Cube. My former colleague Brian Cook, possibly the best researcher in the food movement, could solve any Rubik's Cube problem in less than a minute. The same problem-solving ability allows a good food policy programmer to resolve a food-related problem by synching up moves on all six sides – farms, fisheries, water, health, environment and community, for example. Better still, practice food policy problem-solving skills on Sudoku puzzles. You have to think nine across and nine deep, as in farms, fisheries, home gardens, water, fertilizer, environment, nutrition, economics and transportation. This is what needs to happen with food puzzle-solving – get government or corporate departments focused on agriculture or water or health or community development or job creation to come out of their isolated silos and meet their significant others.

In short, thinking about food as part of an interconnected and interactive system lets us see how tiny food improvements can yield major improvements for all the things food touches. This is what European Union policy calls a multifunctional approach to agriculture. They try to avoid subsidizing farmers as food producers, and instead invest government funds in on-farm activities that contribute to rural vitality (farmers' markets, for example), cultural heritage (recovering 'forgotten vegetables', for example), public education (inviting school classes on a farm tour, for instance) and environmental stewardship (restoring forested lands to store carbon, for example).

Failure to strategize by anticipating the ripple effects or cascading effects of a change almost always creates many-sided problems. These are sometimes called wicked problems. Doctors refer to 'side-effects' of a drug, when what they mean is that they didn't anticipate the direct effects. Calling the problem a side-effect deflects attention from the doctor's mistake, and blames the drug or patient instead. Similarly, organic farmers who hunker down to reduce toxic chemical sprays while growing strawberries need to keep in mind that toxins are also produced when covering the land with plastic sheets that keep weeds from setting down roots, or when making plastic containers to protect the strawberries while they're being hauled across the continent on diesel trucks. Bad systems can foul up the best intentions.

Introducing the food system

But the good food news about the ripple or cascade effect is that the simplest project that co-ordinates system impacts can work wonders. A green roof keeps rainfall out of the sewage overflow, stores the water to evaporate on a hot day when it cools the building, protects the roof from the sun's harsh rays and thereby doubles the roof's life, provides chances for neighbors to work together and build trust while hanging out in the rooftop garden and introduces people to the taste of freshly picked, low-cost, delicious fruits and vegetables.

If I had to explain the persistence of 'food problems' in one sentence, it would be: So-called food problems are caused by putting one narrowly focused government department in charge of the whole food file. All organizations need food animators authorized to bring other departments together so that system benefits can come into view.

Deal with that, and almost any food project works wonders by unlocking dormant opportunities throughout the society, economy and environment. Why? Because food is complex, so combining food and water leads to better solutions for both, just as combining nutrition and exercise more than doubles the impact of working on one or the other alone. Synergy means that the whole is greater than the sum of the parts. Synergy explains why individuals and community groups can leverage such enormous improvements when they link up multi-sided benefits. 'To start the global task to which we are called', says Wisconsin seed expert Jack Kloppenberg, 'we need a specific place to begin, a specific place to stand, a specific place to initiate the small, reformist changes that we can only hope may some day become radically transformative. We start with food.'[9]

Lifecycle costing

Lack of system thinking also means lack of lifecycle thinking. Failure to think ahead in terms of the costs and benefits of a product over the term of its life and afterlife can lead governments to subsidize or support companies that end up doing more harm than good. Governments only started to crack down on tobacco, for example, when they added up the figures and realized that the staggering medical costs paid out for tobacco-related diseases far exceeded the short-term revenues they received from tobacco taxes. The delay in applying the same methodology to food means the real costs and benefits of unhealthy foods are hidden from taxpayers' eyes.

Let's start at the beginning, with examples of food-system impacts on Mother Nature, the source of soil, light, water, air, pollination, warmth and many other no-cost support systems for food production.

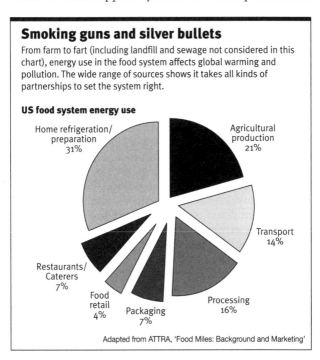

Smoking guns and silver bullets

From farm to fart (including landfill and sewage not considered in this chart), energy use in the food system affects global warming and pollution. The wide range of sources shows it takes all kinds of partnerships to set the system right.

US food system energy use

Home refrigeration/preparation 31%

Agricultural production 21%

Transport 14%

Processing 16%

Packaging 7%

Food retail 4%

Restaurants/Caterers 7%

Adapted from ATTRA, 'Food Miles: Background and Marketing'

Introducing the food system

When the whole food cycle is rolled out – from farm to fart, says England's plain-speaking food expert, Tim Lang – the fossil fuels used in fertilizers, pesticides, tractors, refrigerated trucks and warehouses make for a greenhouse-gassy food system. That's made worse by meat-intensive diets throughout the Global North. It takes 750 million tonnes of fertilizer-intensive grains and 200 million tonnes of pesticide-intensive soybeans to feed the world's 27 billion livestock – judged by many to be the most serious but least talked-about population explosion on the planet – responsible for overloading waterways with manure and clogging the atmosphere with global-warming methane gas from animal farts and burps. Serious analysts, including some associated with the UN's Food and Agriculture Organization and the Bill and Melinda Gates Foundation, say that at least a third of all global warming emissions come from the food industry's meat sector.[10] Ironically, agriculture was almost totally overlooked during the Kyoto process of trying to regulate global warming, and little was done to showcase either problems or solutions that could come from agriculture.

If truth be known, food production is the world's most polluting industry, doing more damage to more territory than logging, mining or heavy industry. The environmental damage it does includes over-fishing, soil degradation, excessive irrigation, and reduction of genetic diversity among farmed animals and plants – all of which are direct threats to future food security, not just to other creatures that share the planet with us.[11]

KPMG, one of the world's leading consultancies, identifies food companies as the world's worst environmental performers. KPMG's 2012 report, *Expect the Unexpected: Building business value in a changing world,* says the food industry inflicts $2.24 of environmental damage for every dollar profit it makes – four times worse than the industrial average. Because the Gross Domestic Product does not identify either costs or benefits related to nature (because no person was paid to produce the assets), loss of soil, species, forested lands and other creators of natural productivity are not reported as debts to be charged against the food system. Count no evil, see no evil, and say no evil – and leave errors embedded deep in the uninvestigated bowels of the system.

Proceed from the impact on nature to the impact on the largest labor force in the world – about 1.1 billion farmers, farm workers and fisherfolk. Agriculture employs 170 million child laborers, more than any other industry[12] – lest anyone ask how food comes to be so cheap when it's outsourced to the Global South. An authoritative 2013 report by Oxfam says the 450 million farmers who supply the 10 biggest food companies account for 60 per cent of the world's poor and 80 per cent of its hungry.[13] Farming has the highest rate of bankruptcy and suicide of any occupation, while farms have the highest rate of workplace accidents, causing 355,000 fatalities a year. A multi-trillion dollar-a-year food industry selling a necessity of life impoverishes more people than any other economic sector.[12]

Although consumers in the Global North unquestion-ably pay a low sticker price for food in this system, the bargain becomes debatable when health impacts are costed out. Too much and too little food are both health problems, and today's food system gets one or the other side wrong for almost half the world's population. As a result of poverty, in large measure caused by low wages for food workers, serious hunger and undernutri-tion are ongoing problems for about one billion people – that's one person in seven on the planet. According to UN statistics for 2013, about 165 million children under five – one quarter of all children under five – are 'stunted' and face lifelong physical and mental disability as a result of undernutrition.[14]

All these children suffer in a world where at least a third of food that's produced is thrown out or otherwise wasted, and where over $40 billion is spent on food marketing that urges people to eat more. Could that money be better spent by helping needy people to eat more?

Overweight and obesity, relatively new and unprecedented problems in world history, affect the health and well-being of some 1.8 billion people. Chronic diseases are now the world's biggest killers, and diseases related to agriculture and food-system products – especially tobacco and alcohol, but increasingly obesity – have the highest impact. Heart specialists say excessive salt – about three-quarters of which comes in processed food, and is not voluntarily and knowingly added by individuals – kills 2.3 million people a year around the world.[15] The US Heart Association says soft drinks cause 180,000 deaths a year.[16] Diets high in salt and fat are linked to chronic diseases that account for 12 per cent of lost years of life.[17] In China, the fifth-biggest country for junk-food outlets, the number of overweight people went from 18 to 100 million between 2005 and 2009, leading one alarmed economist to warn that the costs of chronic disease could 'derail China's growth'.[18] In the US, where almost half the people have one chronic condition and a quarter have at least two, treatment for chronic disease tops out at about one and a half trillion dollars a year.[19] Globally, it will cost $30 trillion to treat chronic disease between 2011 and 2031.[20] This needs to be identified as the overhead cost, the lifecycle cost, of our current food system.

A comprehensive report in 2013 rated the nutrition efforts of the world's 25 biggest food companies. Danone did best, scoring 6.3 out of 10. Unilever scored 6.1 and Nestlé 6.0. PepsiCo got 4.4. Most of the rest scored below 3. None met their own targets to reduce salt, sugar and fat.[17] If $30 trillion of mostly public money will be spent on chronic disease over the next 20 years, someone needs to ask what $30 trillion of public money could do to head off the crisis using food-based remedies.

Failure to do so amounts to a 'regulatory subsidy' to the junk-food industry, making the public pay the lifecycle costs for industry decisions and marketing, just as was done for tobacco a generation ago.

The 'modernist' food system

I refer to the food system that was dominant in the US during and after World War Two, and has since come to dominate much of the globe, as the 'modernist' food system, a term I borrow from architecture. The modernist movement in architecture began early in the 20th century in response to rapid technological change and the availability of new building materials not found in nature – steel, cement and glass. These materials allowed architects to design structures that seemed to defy gravity. Known as 'skyscrapers', these towers were taller, sleeker, airier and lighter than buildings constructed with natural materials such as stone and wood. Architects reveled in the apparent human ability to overcome nature's boundaries. They celebrated the technological innovations that seemed to free us from nature's rules. In many ways, this mentality defined the 20th century. It was also the defining mentality of the modernist food system, a mentality that has transcended politics of the left or the right, cultures of the East or the West, economics of the North and the South. It is the assumption that there will be a technological fix for every problem – the development of additives to prevent food from decaying and make it shelf stable, irradiation to kill bacteria, refrigerated transportation to make it possible to bring food from every corner of the earth, genetically modified plants to bypass natural systems. All of this creates an over-abundance of food, or food-like substances, for some, while impoverishing others, including many of those who actually produce food.

The answer to the problem of overproduction in the modernist food system came in the form of the consumer. This one word, consumer, spells out the crux of the connection between humans and food in today's globally dominant food system. The consumer is a creation of the modern food system. Consumerism emerged at full throttle after World War Two, partly because almost all government leaders and economists of the time believed spending, not saving, was the route to economic health. The first area of expansion for this very innovative model of post-War economic development – the opposite of austerity models dominant since the 1990s – was food production, food processing, food preparation and consumption, as we'll see in the next chapter. A variety of products – from canned foods and TV dinners to dishwashers and large electric fridges – ended the last phases of a household subsistence economy around food, and brought food directly into the mainstream consumer economy. Likewise, farmers stopped saving seeds, composting manure and the like, and became consumers of the inputs of agriculture. Without consumers, the new mass-production food system would have been stillborn.[21]

Such sayings as 'consumer sovereignty' and 'the consumer is king' express the revolution wrought by recasting the economic role of people as consumers, not savers or producers. Oddly, 'consume' was the word previously used to describe overwrought people consumed by passion, or the way houses and people were consumed by fire, or to diagnose people who suffered from tuberculosis or consumption. The model of consumerism was so powerful that systems geared to passive consumption rather than participation became the model for most other activities, from entertainment to government. For example, most public-health advances of the 1940s and 1950s – think vaccination, pasteurization, fluoridation, chlorination, not to mention government-funded medical care – simply required an obedient consumer to engage with an idiot-proofed infrastructure service.

I believe the way out of a food system centered on consumerism lies in the direction of personal agency, social connections and citizen participation. It will require meaningful change in the hearts and minds of individuals, in a wide variety of social institutions and in many government departments. There are signs that a new food system is emerging despite the global dominance of the modernist food system. These signs will be explored in later chapters. But first, let's take a look at how the current food system became entrenched.

1 K Morgan, 'The Urban Foodscape: World Cities and the New Food Equation,' *Cambridge Journal of Regions, Economy and Society*, 3, 2010. **2** N Alexandratos, J Bruinsma, *World Agriculture Towards 2030/2050: the 2012 revision*, ESA Working Paper No 12-03. Jun 2012, FAOSTAT, pp 25, 27. **3** W Davis, *Wheat Belly*, Harper Collins, 2012. **4** A Hamilton, *Squeezed,* Yale University Press, 2009. **5** B Estabrook, *Tomatoland*, Andrews McMeel, 2012. **6** J Baxter, 'Palm oil fuels land grabs in Africa', *Pambazuka News*, 15 Sep 2011; J Rolland, et al, *The Food Encyclopedia,* Robert Rose, Toronto, 2006, p 475; R Wood, *The New Whole Foods Encyclopedia*, Penguin, 1999. **7** IMAP, Food and Beverage Industry Global Report, 2010; this is confirmed in an infographic on food sales in the US: D Thomson, 'Cheap Eats: How America Spends Money on Food,' *The Atlantic*, 8 Mar 2013. **8** T Stuart, *Waste: Uncovering The Global Food Scandal*, Penguin, 2009. **9** J Kloppenberg et al, 'Coming into the Foodshed,' in *Agriculture and Human Values*, 13, 3, 1996. **10** See, for example, H Steinfeld et al, *Livestock's Long Shadow: Environmental Issues and Options* (FAO, Rome: 2006). Also: *The Guardian*, 10 Jan 2013; WorldWatch, 'Farm animal populations continue to grow', *Vital Signs*, 23 March 2012; B and R Vale, *Time to Eat the Do;* FAO Media Centre, 'Cutting Food Waste to Feed the World,' 11 May 2011. **11** T Lang and E Millstone, eds, *The Atlas of Food*, Earthscan 2003. **12** T Lang, 'The Death of Food as We Know It,' *The Ecologist*, Mar 2008; www.planetretail.net **13** Oxfam, *Behind the Brands*, Feb 2013. **14** www.worldhunger.org, 'World Child Hunger Facts'; UNICEF childinfo.org/malnutrition_status.html; UNICEF press release, 'Progress shows that stunting in children can be defeated', 15 Apr 2013. **15** A Mulholland, 'More fatal food: Salty diets leading to 2.3 million deaths each year', *CTV News*, 23 Mar 2013. **16** N Gray, 'Sugary soda linked to 180,000 deaths...', *Food Navigator*, 26 March 2013. **17** Access to Nutrition Index, Global Index 2013. **18** C Chelala, 'How Obesity Can Derail China's Growth', *The Globalist*, 23 Mar 2013. **19** American Association for Clinical Chemistry, Jul 2009, 'Rates of Chronic Disease', is a higher estimate than 'New Infographic Maps the Rise of Chronic Disease', Yahoo Finance, 4 Feb 2013. **20** World Economic Forum, *The Global Economic Burden of Non-Communicable Diseases*, 2011. **21** L Cohen, *A Consumers' Republic*, Vintage 2004.

2 Brave new food

An industrialized food system helped to win World War Two and triumphed on a global scale after the war. Understanding the wartime origins of today's world food system helps to explain the idealistic motivation and rhetoric used by promoters of industrialized food production, the thinking behind many food and agriculture institutions. It also uncovers fundamental flaws that need correcting.

THE ROAD to junk food, rural poverty and agricultural pollution was paved with good intentions. Often criticized as crassly commercial and irresponsible, today's global food system was created in the later period of World War Two as part of an ennobling vision to create a new world of abundance and peace for all. The Washington monument to US President Franklin Roosevelt features many of his inspired wartime statements, when he was preparing for peace. We want 'more than an end to war, we want an end to the beginnings of war', he said. In 1943, Roosevelt summoned Allied leaders to the hot springs in Virginia where he had first learned to stand again after contracting polio. As the springs had been a second chance for him, he saw the coming peace as a second chance for the world to act on the 'most basic of all human needs', if only leaders could learn that world security depended on 'freedom from want and freedom from fear' going hand in hand. Major acclaim at the conference went to Boyd Orr, chief architect of Britain's wartime efforts to keep up morale and strength by ensuring healthy food for all, despite wartime rationing. Having witnessed the improved health, physique and productivity of well-fed people 'has created an entirely new situation which demands economic statesmanship', Orr argued. Such were the deep convictions behind the formation of the future United Nations Food and

Agriculture Organization (FAO) in 1944, led by Boyd Orr, while the War was still being fought.[1]

World War Two was genuinely a world war and a total war. Some 25 million people were killed in battle around the world. The same number of civilians, 25 million, starved to death during the war. About 800 million people, a third of the world's population, faced starvation at the war's end. This was a generation forged by unforgettable experiences as to the centrality of food.[2] The common and optimistic understanding of the period was also that food policy could wage peace, and remove the insecurity and want that bred war. This is why Roosevelt – leader of the most powerful nation to emerge from the war, and deemed voice of the needs of common people in a postwar world – always linked freedom of speech and worship with freedom from want and fear.

The same was true for the United Nations Universal Declaration of Human Rights in 1948, which wove human rights to food and shelter with rights to self-expression and freedom from discrimination into one seamless understanding of human rights. The Declaration was one of the founding documents of the United Nations. Like Roosevelt at the time, but unlike later UN statements, this Declaration simply slips the right to food into a longer list, not particularly noticeable unless the reader knows that later articulations of human rights lacked this integrated view. A high point of post-War idealism, the Declaration remains a touchstone for those who favor food being recognized as a basic human right. As Diana Bronson of Food Secure Canada puts it, 'a young girl going to school without having eaten is not just a tragedy, but a person whose human rights have been violated'.

One of the great 'aha' or 'teachable' moments of food history was based on a momentous transformation the whole world saw during the war – the ability of US farmers, once demand was there, to double food production within five years and produce enough to feed all Americans plus European soldiers during the war. Roosevelt's secretary of agriculture, Claude Wickard, proclaimed that leaps in US food production 'will win the war and write the peace'. He felt 'boundless with the promise of a better world', with 'enough food for the whole world', and with 'more production, more consumption' to create a higher standard of living internationally. His assistant, Milo Perkins, celebrated the first time in history when farmers could grow enough food for all, and make wars over who gets what a thing of the past. 'That's the most important material thing that's happened to the human race since the discovery of fire and the invention of the wheel,' Perkins said.[3]

A legacy of war

This vision of a postwar world was one part American Manifest Destiny; one part wartime adrenalin; one part awe at the achievement, solidarity and purposefulness evoked by mobilization of people, industry and government; one part commitment to build a world fit for returning heroes; and one part worship of Science, which did as much as food to win the war and could do as much to win the peace. There is no denying the wartime mentality linking science, fighting, and triumphant use of food against enemies. 'Recommended Daily Allowances' and 'fortified foods' and food guides, standards on food labels and in government publications to this day, were all developed early in the war to keep people 'strong and healthy' so they could stay 'strong and free'. Likewise, nutrition guides first produced by countries during the war leaned heavily on the iron, calcium and protein in animal protein and fats – two of the four standard food groups – thought necessary for powerful muscles and stamina.

Wartime thinking also invaded an entire generation's attitude about all manner of food, health and science projects, as evidenced by such habit-forming phrases as wars on cancer, drugs, crime, the conquest of poverty, the fight against obesity, aggressive treatment of infections, invasive surgery to destroy disease, antibiotics (literally meaning 'anti-life'). Swords were turned into ploughshares as the wartime arsenal of poisonous gases was re-enlisted for the battle of pesticides and herbicides (from *cide* meaning 'to kill') against weeds and pests. Weapons of choice carried such names as Ambush, Force, Warrior, Battalion, Arsenal, Stalker, Boundary and Machete. 'World War Two did not so much end,' writes Ron Kroese, 'as turn its guns and bombs on the land.'[4]

Wartime needs for prolonged and consistently high performance from soldiers and civilians highlighted the importance of nutrition supporting robust health and national productivity. England even had a Minister of Food to express the importance of that function. However, the opportunity to move food to a health file ended with the war, and food was returned to departments of agriculture, few of which to this day see the health of the population as part of their mandate. This saddles them with a variety of unmanageable conflicts of interest. Agriculture departments are expected to both champion and regulate food producers, for example, an impossibly contradictory assignment. Is the FAO expected to support high prices for fisherfolk or low prices for people who eat fish? Is the US Department of Agriculture supposed to support plentiful corn production on behalf of farmers, or reduced production on behalf of the environment (corn production requires heavy use of pesticides) and public health (corn produces fatty meat and cheap sweetener for pop)?

The continuing war legacy is relevant here because placing food under agriculture only makes sense in relation to war. Making sure food is available for soldiers, who usually need about 4,500 calories a day, has been critical at least since the day when the great French military commander Napoleon pronounced that an army marched on its stomach. In an era of total warfare involving civilians and industry, governments also had to make sure food was available for the home front. Agriculture was best suited to this aspect of national security. Giving food production back to agriculture departments ensured that food processors and processing technologies designed for World War Two continued uninterrupted after the War under government ministries dubbed 'agri-food'. The Second World War created the first mass customer base for processed foods whose composition was seriously altered. For example, 'spam' was a popular army ration because soldiers could eat the meat cold out of the can. Coke and canned orange juice were also mainstays of the US soldier's diet. Instead of phasing out such inferior processed foods after the war emergency, they were rushed into mass production for a home market starved for convenience, especially in North America.

The wartime experience of mobilizing behind Big Science, heavy industry and engineering megaprojects proved a boost for post-War modernist practices. Modernism – premised on the ability of technology and scientific reason to liberate humans from scarcity, ignorance and drudgery – was confirmed during the War by such miracles as antibiotics in medicine, which saved the lives of thousands of wounded soldiers. Big Science and engineering successes inspired people on the left and right of politics in the Global North, as well as leaders of most colonial liberation movements in the Global South, where dams were seen as liberatory technology in countries as different as India and Egypt. The mammoth scale, expense and risk of such projects required as extensive state intervention in the economy as during the war. 'Mixed economies' – marked by major government sponsorship of health, transit, housing, education, hydro development and irrigation infrastructure – were another continuing legacy of the 'command economy' of World War Two.

Industrializing food

During the 1950s and 1960s, what can broadly be called modernism introduced fundamental change at six levels of the food system – most deeply across North America, but setting the standard for change around the world, most immediately in Europe. All six factors were inter-dependent.

First, there was a virtual industrial revolution in the way most food was produced in the Global North. Tractors, combine harvesters and related capital-intensive forms of mechanization became the norm. Science- and engineering-intensive inputs – such as irrigation, chemical fertilizers, petrochemical pesticides and patented hybrid seeds – became standard purchases of commercial farmers. To make maximum use of heavy equipment, farmers increasingly specialized, in grains, livestock, vegetables or fruit. In effect, agriculture became a heavy industry. This industrial revolution in agriculture was made possible by fossil fuels, which powered outdoor machines and generated electricity that could run semi-automated equipment in the middle of a field. The widespread availability of low-cost fossil fuels also eliminated many of the crops and functions farms fulfilled before the advent of fossil fuels. Peri-urban farms no longer grew hay for city or farm workhorses, for example. Nor did they raise animals to sell their fat for soaps and candles or use their manure to fertilize fields. They increasingly specialized in producing food for sale, rather than a range of foods, fibers, fabrics and fuels. They specialized to the extent that they became consumers of inputs, such as fertilizers, which they once produced on-farm. The result was a decline in the farm population – a million Americans a year left the country for the city during the 1950s – that changed the quality of rural life.[5]

Second was an equivalent industrial revolution in household food technology affecting how food was prepared. Gas and electric stoves became the norm, as did large electric refrigerators that could hold a week's groceries. An income revolution enjoyed by working people also allowed many shoppers to purchase labor-saving foods (often called 'meal solutions' today) – everything from sliced bread to prepared cereals to canned and frozen ready-to-reheat meals. A household that once had burlap bags of turnips, flour and potatoes to supply the fixings for a meal now had a pantry full of cans and boxes that could be emptied right into a pot on the stove or put in the oven. By the mid-1950s, TV dinners were packaged in tinfoil, ready to heat and eat. Pizza was available for takeout.

Third was an equivalent commercial revolution, the rise of the supermarket, which affected where people bought food. The car became part of the capital equipment essential to an industrialized household because supermarkets were usually situated further than a walk away from home, and because people bought a week's worth of food to stock a large refrigerator, which required a car to carry the food home. Although super-markets sold fresh food along the outside aisles, their stock in trade, where economies of scale and the power of bulk buying paid off, was in the middle aisles – non-perishable and high-margin household consumer goods, and high-margin processed foods and baked goods. Unlike farmers' markets, which brought farmers and consumers together, supermarkets brought processors and consumers together. The result was a depersonal-ized food system.

Fourth was a transport revolution, courtesy of low-cost fossil fuel, high-tech engineering and massive government expenditures. Freeways, seaways and refrigerated trucks increased the number and volume of foods that could be imported from afar. Once, only non-perishable, expensive and compact foods such as spices could bear the costs of long-distance travel. Then, foods that stored well, such as grains, could make long trips, followed by meat, which could bear the costs of refrigeration because it was quite expensive. Foods that were perishable, bulky and inexpensive couldn't bear the long haul. So market gardeners on the outskirts of major cities supplied these foods in most cities. The transportation revolution of the 1950s removed the last barrier to imported produce, and pushed market farmers out of the farming business and into the business of selling their land to suburban developers. Just as home cooks were deskilled, and food sales were depersonalized, food was delocalized.

Fifth was a revolution in the meals people ate. With increased productivity and hayfields no longer devoted to food for working animals, grain production shot up a third between 1945 and 1965. This super-efficiency created a grain surplus, which for the first time in human history could be used to fatten livestock – a revolution in the diet of animals evolved to eat grass, and a staggering waste of grain, inasmuch as it takes 7 pounds of grain to produce 1 pound of weight gain in beef cattle, 3 pounds of grain to produce 1 pound of weight gain in pigs, and 2 pounds of grain to produce 1 pound of weight gain in poultry.[6] Meat and dairy products became available at a level unprecedented in human history. Americans averaged 138 pounds of meat a year through the 1950s, mostly beef and pork, with chicken a distant third and fish an also-ran. Living off the fat of the land, Americans averaged 33 gallons of whole milk, 8 pounds of cheese and 18 of ice cream over a year, and 44 pounds of added fats and oils such as butter and lard. They also averaged 155 pounds of refined grains, mostly wheat. For my parents and most of the parents I grew up with, all of whom had their full share of hard knocks during the 1930s, these were years that made them feel like kids in a candy store. They indulged their sweet tooth and downed an average 110 pounds of sweetener, mostly cane and beet sugar. Most of this was eaten at home, but the revolution in where people ate can be dated to 1955, when the first McDonald's opened near Chicago,

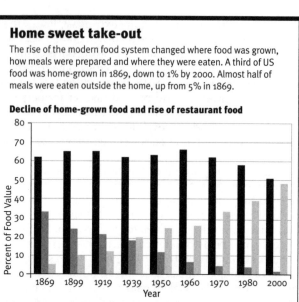

Home sweet take-out

The rise of the modern food system changed where food was grown, how meals were prepared and where they were eaten. A third of US food was home-grown in 1869, down to 1% by 2000. Almost half of meals were eaten outside the home, up from 5% in 1869.

Decline of home-grown food and rise of restaurant food

■ % of food value bought and home-cooked
■ % of food value home-grown and home-cooked
▨ % of food value outside home

Adapted from USDA, ERS, Briefing Rooms, 'Food CPI, Prices and Expenditures: Food and Alcoholic Beverages: Total Expenditures'.

featuring a 15-cent hamburger. More than 400 million were sold in the first decade of the fast-expanding chain, a time when other major fast-service chains also got their start.[7]

The sixth profound change, the best-kept secret of all, was the changing relationship between food and health. Obesity and chronic disease weren't taken seriously until the late 1950s, probably because doctors, like generals, are often refighting the last war, which in the case of health was the war against infectious diseases. A *Life Magazine* issue of March 1954 did raise the specter of the 'Plague of Overweight', but obesity wasn't seriously assessed until the 1959-62 period. The statistics showed that 13.4 per cent of adults were obese and 48 per cent overweight or obese. The figures were sketchy – governments don't measure what they don't think they have to manage. But the rates of heart disease were frightening. In 1963, 805 of every 1,346 deaths were due to cardiovascular disease. Chronic disease officially displaced infectious diseases as the leading cause of death. With some complacency, if not self-congratulation, this transition was often referred to as 'diseases of affluence' rather than diseases of the food system. In 1959, the American Heart Association first recommended that people reduce their levels of dietary cholesterol, careful to use an obscure scientific word no-one knew, rather than to come out and say 'red meat'.[8] After all, this was a medical problem, not a food system problem.

Agribusiness

Agribusiness, like 'better living through chemistry' and 'progress is our product', has a perfect modernist ring. It exemplifies the positioning central to a new food system adapted to a conventional corporate agenda, as distinct from the idealism associated with World War Two.

The word was coined in the mid-1950s by US President Eisenhower's former Assistant Agriculture Secretary, John H Davis, together with Ray Goldberg of the Harvard Business School. Until then, there were no academic courses that envisioned one integrated food industry from farm to table, an industrial chain in which farm products became 'inputs'. The first Harvard agribusiness seminar for business executives was in 1956, and Goldberg takes pride that every US Department of Agriculture (USDA) secretary since has taken the course. To keep up with bulk orders from centralized agribusinesses, Agriculture Secretary Ezra Taft Benson told farmers they had no choice but to use economies of scale to spread the costs of expensive inputs over more output. So, 'get big or get out', he told farmers. Industrialized and scientific became synonyms for corporate food production.[9]

The term 'agribusiness' deserves an A+ for brilliance in framing a new food agenda. Most obviously, it severs agriculture from culture and integrates it directly with business. Moreover, it excludes many key elements of a food system from view. Most people now think of the food supply chain as equivalent to the food system, even though the supply chain excludes a wide range of occupations that work with food, including people who fish or forage, or people who make food utensils or kitchen equipment or do kitchen renovations, or people who work on water issues, or people who work in the health field, all of which have critical implications for food production and preparation. Privileging business as the one group built in at the defining stage precludes other ways of configuring food than as a commodity for sale.

Supermarket surge

The supermarket burst on the food scene with modernist hype and classic modernist building materials: lots of glass, chrome, high-powered lights, straight, narrow rows. Energy waste is standard with modernist designs, expressed in huge open freezers at the store. Standard supermarket props seem to come from modernist design checklists: bright packages, shiny, perfect produce; no odor of actual food; no sign of feathers or blood that might suggest the food's origin; no yelling, hawking, bantering or greeting; no haggling over price; no buskers; no public property not totally controlled by the owner; and minimal artistry or enchantment that might distract from buying.

Abundance is the first message of the supermarket. Virtually unlimited consumer choice is the second message. Convenience is the third, which is why supermarkets are usually attached to parking lots, and why supermarkets undermine the business diversity of main streets with their effort to promote one-stop shopping. Affordability was the fourth (but has probably moved up to first under the pressure of discounters since the 1990s). In the UK, supermarkets almost doubled their share of the market during the 1960s, taking most sales from independents; they did not take from co-ops until the 1990s. In the US, supermarket share of food sales soared from 14.9 per cent in 1948 to 55 per cent in 1972, growth that mainly took from mom and pop groceries, specialty stores and home delivery services. By the 1970s, supermarkets became pivotal players in the food industry and food system, not only selling food but using their bulk buying power to reorganize the supply chain, forcing companies to amalgamate to meet their bulk order for chain-wide sales, even if that meant destruction of a region's local food capacity. Rather than work with members of the supply chain as partners, supermarkets gave processors a take-it-or-leave-it price point and let them figure out how to push the problem down the line and do what had to be done. This was a true retail revolution, as Tony Winson, one of the first authors to identify their role, has noted.[10]

Full-on, abundance-spreading modernism flourished during the 1950s and 1960s, when global politics were defined by two factors. First, the Cold War between the Soviet Union and the US pressured both to vie for support from other countries by promising to help them meet their goals. Second, the end of European colonialism, something the US insisted on as a condition of helping Europe recover from the devastation of World War Two, opened possibilities for former Asian, African and South American countries to participate in 'development'. There were 'three worlds of development', it was said – the American and European First World, the Soviet Second World, and the increasingly restive Non-Aligned Movement, which came to be known as the Third World. Strategists for both US- and

Brave new food

Soviet-style modernist food systems tried to jockey for political and economic advantage in this arena.

The Green Revolution

During the Cold War, the US had several reasons to support increases to the farm productivity of the Third World (known as the 'Global South' since the end of the Cold War). First, the US thought this was the way to solve hunger problems that caused mass unrest: by 'growing the pie' so there was more for everyone, rather than fighting over slices of a smaller pie. Second, the US hoped to document the superiority of US production methods over Soviet ones. Third, it hoped to capitalize on sales of industrial farm inputs (tractors, fertilizers, and so on) used by 'high input, high yield' Third World farmers who saw their farms as private investment vehicles rather than community holdings.

High-input, high-yield agriculture came across as dull as dishwater as a campaign slogan. Then a US government publicity flak came up with the name 'Green Revolution', hoping this spin on high-yield farming contrasted nicely to Red (Communist) Revolution. The Johnny Appleseed of the Green Revolution was Norman Borlaug, who received the Nobel Prize and scores of other top honors for his contributions to peace and development through high-yield farming. As a youth during the 1930s Depression, Borlaug worked on public works projects for the unemployed. He took up agricultural research when he saw the connection between hunger and war. 'You can't build a peaceful world on empty stomachs and human misery,' he explained. Websites dedicated to Borlaug's reputation commonly claim that he has saved the lives of one billion people who would have starved to death without his high-yield seeds.

Borlaug's first big project was sponsored by the Rockefeller Foundation in Mexico during the 1940s. In a country where the vast majority of peasants were indigenous peoples who grew corn, Borlaug developed a breed of wheat that resisted disease and produced significant yields, though requiring more irrigation than would ever be available to indigenous farmers in drier areas. Borlaug's most famous work was in India during the 1950s and 1960s, where he developed high-yielding grains. His last work prior to his death in 2009 was with the Gates and Rockefeller foundations in Africa. Some of Borlaug's critics see significance in his longstanding connection to the Rockefeller Foundation (endowed with money made in the oil industry), given the high fossil-fuel needs fostered by his high-input agriculture strategies.[11]

Modernist building designers were famous for saying that 'form follows function'. They despised wasting expense on frills that didn't add to a building's prime purpose. Borlaug felt the same way about plants. Their job was to increase yield for humans, the only species that counted in his calculations. He believed that many grain plants wasted too much energy on tall stems that did nothing but stand tall. In Mexico, he selected wheat plants with dwarf stems, which boosted grain output. In India, he worked on rice that matured quickly, producing an extra crop on the same space each year.

Yields skyrocketed under Borlaug's demonstration of what US-sponsored science could accomplish by overcoming the old ways. Indian rice output doubled almost overnight. By 2001, India grew 70 million tons of Green Revolution wheat, enough to feed everyone in India 2,800 calories a day. Instead of going to the one Indian in five who is chronically hungry, however, the surplus grain went to a 60-million-ton stockpile, some destined for export. Clearly, more than food production increases were needed to end hunger.

Borlaug personified the passion of modernist idealists who believed the problem of world hunger could be solved by growing more food. Most governments and corporate foundations agree with Borlaug's view on the challenge, and invest their funds in schemes that can boost food production, especially genetic engineering, the controversial practice of transferring DNA from one plant or animal to another, ostensibly to increase yield by making the plant resistant to certain pesticides.

An assessment of Borlaug's relevance today requires a critical look at the deep, almost unconscious, bias of a food system that came out of World War Two – a time when hunger was the undisputed health crisis facing the world, and when such a huge proportion of the world's population were farmers that distribution of any food produced was not a challenge.

Today's world is an entirely different place. More people face health threats from obesity than from hunger, and do not need more access to low-cost grains. Those who confront hunger will benefit more from innovative ways of distributing food, already produced in amounts sufficient for the world's needs. The Borlaug debate needs to be given a rest so we may face up to the challenges of today's world to which modernist thinking about food doesn't seem capable of responding.

Payback time

Since 2000, the Green Revolution piper has had to be paid. Short-sighted promotion of short-stemmed plants left less fodder for livestock, and less straw for composting manure for fertilizer, depleting the land of complex micronutrients. Some fields were degraded from salt deposits in irrigation water, which is usually hard water, unlike salt-free soft rainwater that might be conserved better by paying attention to soil rather than seeds, since well-aerated and organic soils can hold more water than soils relying on chemical fertilizers.

Community relations in many areas subject to Green Revolution methods have deteriorated as a result of infighting over access to scarce inputs, such as well water. For example, suicide rates of the Punjab's many indebted farmers are nightmarishly high; the Green

Revolution, argues Devinder Sharma, one of India's leading agriculture critics, 'has not only turned sour, it has now turned red' with blood. *The Economist*, usually a fan of scientific bells and whistles, pronounced the Green Revolution in the Punjab, India's breadbasket, to be 'in retreat' and a 'catastrophe'. Two reports from the state government of the Punjab – formerly a major fan of the Green Revolution – have recommended a return to pre-Green Revolution farming methods.[12]

Feeding the world

Food aid was another insignia of the modernist approach to providing food for those in need. Following World War Two, the US was the leading force on the world stage, and used its resources to confront its Cold War enemies in the Soviet Union and China, and assist its Cold War allies elsewhere. About $13 billion in US aid through the Marshall Plan helped Europe to recover from the devastation of war between 1947 and 1952. On the heels of this success, the US donated billions in food aid to governments it deemed in need of assistance, usually non-Communist governments or countries in international hotspots.

Food aid was a showpiece of US generosity but, like most charitable programs before and since, had more than its share of patronizing errors. The US felt called on to 'feed the world', a problematic term in two respects. First, cattle are fed, babies are fed, but dignified human adults eat, and do not like to think of themselves as being fed. Second, it is not the assignment of any nation to feed the world, but to help people become self-reliant and produce more of their own food. Third, it is unethical to put a price on charitable offerings to feed others in desperate need. Many analysts believe that US food aid played the role of the Trojan horse in Greek mythology, encouraging countries to let down their guard until it was too late. It happened too often that farmers in a country receiving aid were bankrupted by competition with underpriced US imports, and had to leave their farms to find work in the city, or that people in other countries had to accept food donations that were part of the American diet, not theirs. Once a society depended on imports, it was on the commercial treadmill. US aid, says leading food system analyst Harriet Friedmann, disrupted subsistence economies by 'widening and deepening capitalist relations within the world economy, by shifting vastly more of the world's population away from direct access to food and incorporating it instead into food markets.' Turning food into a traded commodity, she says, was 'a crucial aspect of proletarianization' of formerly subsistence economies turned into workshops of cheap manufactured goods for export.

Until food aid was developed, most North American grains were sold into Europe. Countries in Asia, Africa and South America remained self-sufficient in grains before the Second World War. After the War, the US government subsidized American grain farmers to export as much surplus as possible. In 1950, for example, over 60 per cent of US exports were financed as aid. By 1956, US aid accounted for a third of the world wheat trade, much of it directed to countries where governments encouraged people to leave their farms and work in factories. By 1968, poor countries of the world received 78 per cent of US exports. In a major flip of the traditional roles of colonial and industrialized economies, wheat and other grains – crops that could take full advantage of mechanized farm equipment to which wealth gave access – became the export products of industrialized countries of the Global North. This flip blocked two standard routes to economic development of former colonies – either through export agriculture, selling crops they grew efficiently, or through import substitution, protecting start-up effort to produce for the home market.

The ongoing legacy of US food aid, Friedmann argued

Happy Days highlights

1946: launch of Tupperware, frozen french fries, instant mashed potatoes
1947: Marilyn Monroe named first Artichoke Queen
1950: the first Dunkin Donuts, Minute Rice and Kraft sliced processed cheese
1952: Sugar Frosted Flakes, 29-per-cent sugar
1953: Kraft Cheeze Whiz, TV dinners and Sugar Smacks, 56-per-cent sugar
1954: Burger King founded
1955: McDonald's first franchise opens, instant oatmeal invented
1957: margarine outsells butter

Source: foodreference.com/html/html/food-history.html

in 1982, is colonial dependence on high-priced grain imports. This proved prophetically true in the years following 2008, when the high price of US wheat exports forced many in low-income countries to go without food.[13] In 2013, US President Barack Obama acknowledged the legitimacy of food-movement critics of US aid policies and moved to donate more money and less grain to countries in need, allowing them the option to buy more food from local farmers and thereby increase national self-reliance.[14]

Speeches trumpeting high-yield agriculture are still the comfort food of choice at US food industry get-togethers. At a conference on production agriculture in Chicago in 2007, economist David Oppedahl reviewed the signposts of progress: farm output has more than doubled since 1948, despite huge reductions in cropland, farm workers and farmers; soy and corn output has doubled since 1964; each farmer increased hourly output 12-fold between 1950 and 2000; food prices since 1948 rose at less than half the rate of general prices; the farmer's share of the food dollar in 1997 was 21 cents.[15]

Brave new food

Many defenders of pesticides or genetically engineered seeds dress their cause with rhetoric from the era of World War Two modernism. One of these is Dennis Avery, the Hudson Institute author of *Saving the Planet with Pesticides and Plastic: the Environmental Triumph of High Yield Farming*. Others wax eloquent about genetic engineering as the savior of poor farmers and consumers, despite widespread evidence to the contrary. There is evidence, for example, that yields over time are better with organic, that the low-input costs and demands of traditional seeds are more helpful to low-resource farmers, and that current genetically engineered crops – such as corn, soy, canola and cotton – yield little health or environmental benefit and little promise of adaptability to the rigorous demands of agriculture in an era of global warming.[16]

Modernism loses its groove

The spell of post-War modernism was challenged during the 1970s. In 1971, a strategic assessment of the economy led President Richard Nixon to promote 'green power' as part of the US bid to become 'breadbasket of the world'. This was premised on the US becoming a worldbeater in the arena of cheap agriculture. The subsequent drive to boost subsidized exports of US grains, as sociologist Philip McMichael has documented, was no longer about sharing abundance and helping others to develop. It used poor countries as a dumping ground for grain surplus and a source of cheap imported manufactured goods.[17] Other cracks in the modernist consensus were revealed in 1974, during the high-profile US-sponsored international conference on famine, hunger and runaway food prices. Classics of the global food system analysis were written in response to the hoopla of that event. Susan George's *How the Other Half Dies* and Frances Moore Lappé's *Food First: Beyond the Myth of Scarcity* were precocious in their time and still read well today, setting out key elements of the global agenda for a different food system model. During the 1970s, modernism lost its hegemonic groove and became controversial. Other food strategies seemed possible.

The bloom came off the rose in 1976, when the US opposed a UN-sponsored International Covenant on Economic, Social and Cultural Rights, which reaffirmed 'the fundamental right of everyone to be free from hunger'. The US-sponsored International Covenant on Civil and Political Rights of the same year made a vague reference to everyone having 'the inherent right to life', without a reference to food or other human essentials. Preparing for the 2008 celebration of the Universal Declaration of Human Rights' 60th anniversary, Louise Arbour, UN High Commissioner for Human Rights, complained that the assumption that prosperity will look after the poor 'is a misguided view of what human rights are about.' She said that 'there's no reason to assume that prosperity will transform itself naturally into any form of social justice'.[18]

Fast forward to 2008. Thanks to approximately $50 billion a year in crop subsidies, the US Farm Bill influences the fundamentals of world agriculture and food practices. The direct crop payments, in order of money received, go to support corn, wheat, cotton, soybeans, rice, sorghum, barley and peanuts. Several things stand out in this list. All are export crops, and almost all give the US global price leadership, determining what unsubsidized smallholder farmers will be able to charge outside the US, in countries that cannot match US subsidies. All US-subsidized crops can be produced with high levels of mechanization, reducing the disadvantage that the US might face in competition with low-wage economies, but also reducing the jobs created by public expenditure. These subsidies actually encourage the hollowing out of the countryside, in the US and elsewhere, by artificially encouraging large mechanized farm operations.

Since all the subsidized crops deplete water and soil nutrients, subsidizing them violates a basic principle of resource conservation. Many of the subsidized crops, especially corn and cotton, require high levels of toxic pesticides, thereby subsidizing the poisoning of water tables. At least four – corn, soy, barley and wheat – are primarily intended for livestock and production of low-cost meat. Subsidizing these grains is a way of laundering government money to products and companies that few people would think worthy of subsidies: beer from barley, pop from corn syrup, ethanol fuel from corn, meat from raising livestock on corn and soy instead of grass and hay. By subsidizing these crops, the US government lowers the cost of practices that are harmful to health and the environment – the opposite of sound economic planning. No fruit and vegetables, no alternative crops, and no crops grown for local markets are on this list.[19]

The original modernist vision of the 1940s has been stripped of almost all but the rhetoric of US influence over global thinking and practice around food issues. The notions and institutions of combining science, planning, government commitment, public co-operation and wide-ranging human rights were dismantled during the 1990s, with the formation of the World Trade Organization. All that remains of the original commitment is high-production agriculture. A system which hoped to provide bread for all now strives to live on grains alone.

1 'Final Act of the United Nations Conference on Food and Agriculture,' Hot Springs, Virginia, 1943; Nobelprize.org. 'The Nobel Peace prize 1949 Lord Boyd Orr'. **2** L Collingham, *The Taste of War*, Penguin, 2012. **3** 'Hunger, Cover Story,' *Time*, 21 July 1941. **4** See, for example, A Blay-Palmer, *Food Fears* (in press, 2008); S Dean, 'Children of the Corn Syrup,' in *Believer*, Oct 2003; Ron Kroese, 'How Did We Get Here: The Culture of Agribusiness,' in *Conscious Choice*, May 1999. **5** R Albritton, 'Two Great Food Revolutions: The Domestication of Nature and the Transgression of Nature's Limits' in M Koc et al, eds, *Critical Perspectives in Food Studies*, Oxford, 2012. **6** nin. tl/106nRM8 **7** USDA, Agriculture Fact Book, 'Profiling Food Consumption in America,' pp 15-20; V Smil, 'Eating Meat: Evolution, Pattern and Consequence,' pp 609, 617, nin.tl/10x7AD4 **8** R Utz, 'Obesity in America,

1960-2000', PAA 2005; Weight Control Information Network, US Department of Health and Human Services, Overweight and Obesity Statistics; J Komios, M Brabec, 'The evolution of BMI values of US adults: 1982-1986,' VOX, 31 Aug 2010; National Heart, Lung and Blood Institute, Fact Book, Disease Statistics. **9** 'The Evolution of Agribusiness,' in HBS@Work Faculty Interview; nin.tl/106nGAw **10** T Lang and M Heasman, *Food Wars*, Earthscan, 2004, p 166; 'Food CPI, Prices and Expenditures: Sales of Food at Home by Type of Outlet,' in *USDA/ERS Briefing Room*, 2 July 2007; T Winson, *The Intimate Commodity*, Garamond Press, 1992. **11** R Patel, 'The Long Green Revolution', in *The Journal of Peasant Studies,* 40:1, 2013. **12** V Smil, *Feeding the World*, MIT Press, 2001; R Thurow and J Solomon, 'An Indian Paradox: bumper harvests and rising hunger,' *Wall Street Journal*, 25 Jun 2004; nin.tl/10x7ll7; V Shiva, *The Violence of the Green Revolution*, Zed, 1991; D Sharma, 'The Collapse of Green Revolution,' at www.stwr.net/content/view/116/37/; 'Chemical generation,' at *Economist.com* 24 Sep 2007; 'Need to stop disastrous cropping pattern: Report,' at www.punjabenvironment.com 27 Aug 2007. **13** H Friedmann, 'The Political Economy of Food', in *American Journal of Sociology*, 88, 1982. **14** T Rosenberg, 'When Food Isn't the Answer to Hunger,' *New York Times*, Opinionator, 24 Apr 2013; globalfoodpolitics, 'A Long-Overdue Change to US Food Aid,' 15 Apr 2013. **15** http:// midwest. chicagofedblogs.org-/archives/200710/ **16** See, for example, D Pimental, 'Impacts of Organic Farming on the Efficiency of Energy Use in Agriculture', *The Organic Center*, Aug 2006; JM Smith, *Seeds of Deception*, Yes Books, 2003. **17** P McMichael, *Development and Social Change*, Pine Forge Press, 2000, p 64. **18** G Kent, 'Food is a Human Right,' foodnews, 22 Jun 2004, archived at www.foodforethought.net; F Williams, 'UN drive for economic and social rights,' *Financial Times* 8 Jan 2008. **19** L Etter and G Hitt, 'Farm Lobby Beats Back Assault on Subsidies,' *Wall Street Journal*, 27 Mar 2008, pp 1, 12.

3 The high cost of cheap food

The rise of cheap food, the decline of Northern manufacturing and the tragedy of Southern 'development' during the 1970s were all of the same piece. This chapter shows that a lot more than bad diets came from the rise of junk food. Cheap food comes at a great cost to health, the environment, community and economic well-being.

I SAW THE LIGHT on abundance at seven o'clock on a sunny August morning on my first day back volunteering at Stowel Lake Farm on Salt Spring Island, a little piece of paradise on Canada's west coast. It was my second season, so I knew the breakfast routine. I walked about 30 meters from our cabin and started picking from a wild patch of juicy blackberries. I picked two cereal bowls of berries while standing in one place, thanks to a little trick for seeing more than meets the eye. Gently bobbing the branches, I could see berries formerly lurking in the shadows, as plump and juicy as any. There should be a parable of the right mix of light, shadow and angle for berry picking, I thought. Abundance is all around us; we just have to look for it in the right light.

Later that same day, I learned the awful truth about blackberry bounty when I went into town and saw the headline in the regional farm paper. I suddenly saw the wealth of perfect berries through the eyes of commercial growers. The front page story said berry producers across the Pacific Northwest expected their worst season in 15 years – unless a cold snap or heat wave finished off Serbian berries. Otherwise, markets glutted by Serbian berries from thousands of kilometers away would destroy the price of fresh and local berries. In the eyes of farmers facing global rivals, nature's bounty is a curse that triggers price collapse.

Like everybody in the food sector, berry farmers

are caught in the vortex of cheap food. Cheap food is the Tyrannosaurus Rex in the room that never gets discussed in polite company. A cheap food policy is never an election issue or subjected to a formal vote in legislatures. Cheap food just goes without saying – like it goes without saying that migrant workers without basic rights do the heavy lifting at fruit and vegetable farms, or that ships transport cheap food using the cheapest and most polluting fuels, or that WTO trade rules override UN human rights declarations.

The origins of cheap food

Some trace back the model for a cheap food policy to the bread and circuses of the ancient Roman Empire. But the modern prototype comes from the dawn of British industrialism, also a time of imperial conquest that brought cheap sugar, tea, coffee and, later, white bread within reach of early factory workers. They got four boosts from the new foods: a jolt of caffeine to send them off to work alert (quite a change from the effect of the traditional breakfast drink, ale); a quick hit of energy to fuel their bodies for the work shift; a fast meal of bread and jam munched on the way out the door; and perhaps the cheap thrill of belonging to an empire on top of the world.

Cheap food had a gigantic ripple effect. Cheap sugar came from enslaving Africans and transporting them to plantations in the Caribbean, where the original inhabitants were removed to make way for the conquerors. Cheap tea came from subjugating India. Cheap grains drove the opening of the North American frontier west, driving out the original inhabitants, largely to create space for immigrants driven off their land in Europe by competition with cheap grain from the Americas. By reducing a major cost item in the budget of working people, cheap food substituted for other social policies that could have sustained urban and factory life – minimum wages or social housing, for example, as was done in parts of continental Europe where a more complex 'welfare state' evolved. Cheap food allowed these expenses to be outsourced to disadvantaged people in other countries who bore the burdens of delivering cheap product.[1]

Finding the control room of Britain's cheap food policy is impossible. Was it slavery that delivered cheap food? Was it the triumph of free trade during the 1840s and the subsequent 'informal empire' that roped farmers in the Americas into supplying cheap grains? Cheap food was a complex more than a policy. Perhaps the point to make is that no-one was ever so ill-considered as actually to conceive and plan a system with so many negative consequences. But cheap food did come out of a culture of mechanistic utilitarianism, which ran rampant during industrialism. The industrialized body needed 'fuel' for its motor, and that's what cheap food provided.

Cheap food would not have played as well in a society where the body is understood as a temple, needing life energy, *prana* or *chi* from the universe. Cheap food took hold in a public culture divorced from understanding that food was an essential of life – as essential to cultural heritage, rural survival, economic planning, ecological biodiversity and spiritual connectivity as it was to delivering work energy to the employer. A cheap food complex goes deep into a society – one reason why it's no easy matter to change.

Cheap food in the 20th century

Major elements of the British cheap food complex remained in force in Britain and its settler colonies in Australia, New Zealand and North America throughout the 1800s and 1900s. But cheap food took on renewed importance during the early 1970s when it became pivotal to a major restructuring of the US and world economy. Pioneering analysis by Cornell University sociologist Philip McMichael traces the change to the team around US President Richard Nixon, who foresaw the need to reorient the US economy. It was decided that the US could lead in exports of high-technology manufacturing, such as munitions, and in capital-intensive food exports, such as wheat, corn and cotton. Other products were best made by countries with cheaper and more disciplined workers, cheaper and less strict environmental regulations, and cheaper and less democratically checked politicians.[2]

This was a fundamental rethink of the power base of economies. The older, more traditional colonialism set up a dependency 'debt trap' which locked colonial hinterlands into exporting low-cost raw materials to the imperial center, which then exported more expensive manufactured goods to the colonies, indebting them again. By contrast, the post-1970s schema valued former colonies for their low wages, strong work ethic, docile unions and weak environmental standards – all disappearing from the West at the time, and all ideal for 1970s-era manufacturing. So next-generation factories went south, leaving behind the low-wage service sector, which had no choice but to stay close to the customers it served.

In this scenario, farmers in the Global North took advantage of large farms, advanced technology and public infrastructure to export cheap grains, dairy and meat to the Global South. Workers in neocolonial factories of the Global South got by on low wages by eating low-cost food grown in the formerly industrialized Global North. Poorly paid consumers in the Global North got manufactured imports made by underpaid labor in the Global South, thanks to a constant influx of new factory workers, driven off their land by cheap imports of food from the Global North. Cheap food rejigged social and economic structures as well as trade patterns of both the Global North and Global South.

By 1994, a year before the World Trade Organization (WTO) came into effect, just 2 per cent of US farms accounted for 64 per cent of world trade in corn, 40 per cent of soy, 36 per cent of wheat, 33 per cent of cotton and 17 per cent of rice. By 2003, countries still commonly referred to as industrial exported $321 billion worth of foodstuffs, 74 per cent of their agricultural earnings; by comparison, countries of the Global South, usually depicted as pre-industrial, exported $138 billion worth of foodstuffs, only 19 per cent of their agricultural earnings.[3]

The changeover to a political economy based on a global swap of cheap food and cheap manufactured goods coincided with the stormy geopolitics of the early 1970s, when resource shortages were confounded by cataclysmic rhetoric and confrontational politics. World population, edging close to four billion in 1970, was often referred to as the 'population bomb'. A new leadership from governments of formerly colonized countries said the world was divided between North and South, haves and have-nots, and declared themselves a 'third world', no longer pawns of the first and second worlds of Capitalists and Communists. Arab countries jacked up oil prices in 1973 to retaliate against Western support for Israeli expansion, and the ensuing 'oil shock' pushed up the price of most products. The world economy was stuck in 'stagflation', a double whammy of unemployment and inflation. The modernist era of continuous progress seemed to hit a wall, which a classic report in 1972 called *The Limits to Growth*.

Food wasn't far from the storm center. The global harvest declined in 1972, followed by horrific famines in Ethiopia and Bangladesh and food shortages in about 20 countries. Emergency grain reserves dropped to 26 days' supply. Wheat prices shot up sixfold, affecting the price of milk and meat, both of which are dependent on low-cost grains. Oil price increases had the same impact on costs of fertilizer, pesticides and irrigation – the three pillars of modernist high-input, high-production agriculture. In order to ensure food for the home population, the US and several European countries banned or limited food exports.

For power brokers such as Henry Kissinger, US President Richard Nixon's Secretary of State, this turmoil was a crash course in international politics as an exercise in raw economic power. 'Control the oil and you control entire nations,' Kissinger would say, with an eye to the Arab monopoly over low-cost oil. 'Control the food and you control the people,' he'd continue, confident of US supremacy in that field. Food became the US checkmate to the strategic power of Arab oil. 'Hungry men listen only to those who have a piece of bread,' Nixon's Agriculture Secretary Earl Butz said. 'Food is a tool. It is a weapon in the US negotiating list.' The term 'food security' was coined during this period, when food was understood as strategic to national security and economic security.

Another area of reinvention related to women's rights. The early British version of cheap food predated women having the right to vote and the era when married women worked outside the home. But the 1970s US sequel adapted to new realities. Cheap processed foods were depicted as a convenience revolution that liberated women from the drudgery of unpaid housework. With processed and take-out foods to help, women no longer had to stay at home just to cook dinner. This shift fitted perfectly with the shift across the Global North to a labor-intensive service and office workforce after the 1970s, a de-industrialized workforce in which a male no longer earned a 'living wage' to support his family. Once families needed two full-time incomes to manage, something had to give, and that was food preparation. Cheap prepared and take-out foods came to the rescue of both two-income and single-parent families, in which adults worked more hours outside the home than they did before the cheap food revolution that liberated them. The 'value added' was convenience, a word that put a positive spin on the fact that two-income families were under increasing time pressures. Processed, prepared and take-out meals became the ultimate in supporting cheap labor, because they allowed two parents to earn enough to support a family that one paid and one unpaid parent had supported before.

Food itself was reinvented by the 1970s cheap food revolution. The reduced cost of meals that came with more processing and convenience was made possible in part by reductions in the amount of the food dollar that went to farmers. US farmers received 37 cents on the food dollar in 1973, but less than 20 cents after 2000. The ability of processors to deliver prefab food without raising prices raises the question: is cheap food cheap despite being processed, or because it is processed? Readers of Michael Pollan's *The Omnivore's Dilemma*, will appreciate that processed food is cheap precisely because it uses the multiple personalities of corn to stand in for functions and tastes otherwise performed by more costly real foods. The more processing, the more corn, the less money spent on actual food, the cheaper the meal – that's the economic recipe.

That's why grains and meat, not fruit and vegetables, remain the foundation of a cheap food diet. Grains can be converted to cheap meat by feeding them to livestock penned up in factory barns. And grains can be stretched so that four cents of corn provide four dollars of cornflakes, 27 cents of potatoes cost $3.40 in potato chips and 2.6 cents of corn provides four dollars' worth of corn chips. Fruits and vegetables, which should be the foundation of a healthy diet, are not the foundations of a 'value-added' processed food industry. By 2002, world sales of processed foods came to $3.2 trillion.[4]

Corporate concentration

There's another major difference between the old and the new in cheap food. The original British version of cheap food happened when food retailers and processors were small-scale and regional, and when canning, then less than 50 years old, was about as far as food manufacturing went. By the 1970s, a handful of global oligopolies could produce, transform and retail a wide range of foods across continents. By 2004, 15 corporations controlled almost a fifth of all packaged foods. Backstage, the same pattern of corporate concentration typifies all players in the food chain – except for food producers and consumers, who are on their own when they face these conglomerates at opposite ends of the food system. Ten seed companies control seeds, for example, while five trading companies control grain sales, ten pesticide companies control pesticides, and so on. Yet despite the clout of these seemingly powerful input manufacturers and processors, the shift to cheap food coincided with an inter-corporate power shift from input suppliers and processors to retailers. After the 1970s, supermarkets controlled the pecking order. Since they controlled access to customers, they told processors what price points to meet for what quantities, and the processors passed the burden down the line to farmers. Monopolies with bulk purchasing power became the enforcers of cheap food. However, since the era of cheap food, the norm has been cut-throat competition among monopolies vying for market share by discounting. Cheap food controls monopolies, not the other way around. Indeed, cheap food creates monopolies because the only way companies can survive low margins is with huge volumes. Monopolies become bigger because volume is about the only survival factor they can influence.[5]

The cheap food system works on a virtuous circle from Hell – technology and infrastructure allows farmers from the Global North to sell cheap grains, meats and dairy products into the Global South; low-cost imported food keeps poorly paid Southern factory workers alive; a continuous flow of fresh recruits from the countryside to work in Southern factories keeps wages low after workers lost their farms to competition from cheap food imports; cheap manufactured goods from the Global

The high cost of cheap food

South sell to low-waged Northern workers. Economic analyst Greg Albo calls it 'competitive austerity', which draws companies and countries into methods that eventually lead to mutually assured destruction. 'Competition in the new global economy' has become a stock phrase that covers up the reality that we have more food than we know what to do with because the only thing we know how to do is compete.[6]

Cheap food depends on government-funded aid to make Northern grains and dairy available to the Global South. It relies on public subsidies for university research, energy and transportation. It takes export subsidies for grains, which are exported as stand-alone products and as feed for livestock. Cheap food depends on aggressive campaigns by Northern governments to lower protective barriers against imports in the Global South. It relies on government tolerance of global monopolies with power to determine patterns of international trade, because most international trade is simply a transfer of goods within the supply chain of one corporation. Finally, cheap food relies on a food culture divorced from tradition and parenting, featuring ingredients such as sugar, grains, dairy and meat, prepared for heating and eating. Thanks to the interplay of such factors, the US and Europe competed in 2003 for top spot in exports of cereals, meat and milk; the US led the world with oilseeds, citrus and fibers, while Europe took a big lead on sugar – the opposite of what might be expected from industrialized countries.[7]

Bono and Bob: the fallacy of 'trade, not aid'

Like the invisible hand of a market that went unrecognized until Adam Smith named its power, the hand behind cheap food awaits its Adam Smith. Cheap food has avoided recognition as the defining systemic force behind controversies about global food, trade, health, equity and environment since the 1980s. For instance, the cheap food complex did not get discussed in *Our*

Common Future, a landmark publication of the World Commission on Environment and Development in 1987, best known for the phrase 'sustainable development'.

Nor has awareness of this cheap food trading pattern been raised in many public policy debates since. It certainly can't compete with the popularity of a famous one-liner dropped by some unknown person on the best way to help poor people in the developing world. Give a man a fish and you feed him for a day, the line went, but teach him to fish, and you feed him forever. The advice sounds so patronizing today that it's funny. The original advice was a metaphor – I doubt anyone believed that poor people didn't know how to fish – that came out of the development era of the 1950s, when it was thought all countries would develop, become mature, self-reliant and equal through productive work and trade. No-one would give such advice in today's world. Why give any fish to poor people when you can give them corndogs, and sell the lean and healthy fish protein to rich people? Teach a factory ship to fish, and it can feed Northerners forever, is today's advice.

Those hooked on the fish stories go for the idea that 'trade, not aid' will help countries climb out of poverty. Those promoting barrier-free trade include famous rockers such as Bono and Bob Geldof, associated with the compelling Make Poverty History campaign of 2005. The media gave full play to Bono and Geldof's campaign to pressure a meeting in Scotland of leaders of the world's eight wealthiest countries. Geldof said three policies could make poverty history and fix Africa's problems 'in 10 seconds' – cancel paralyzing debts to international bankers, raise foreign aid, and end the subsidies and barriers that block African exporters from financing development through trade, not aid.

I was at a conference in Dublin on peak oil and food security at the time, and asked quite a few people for their thoughts on Bono and Geldof. If increased trade solved anything, replied Darrin Qualman, former

The high cost of cheap food

Research Director of Canada's National Farmers' Union, Canadian farmers would be the poster children. They increased foreign grain sales from $10.9 billion in 1988 to $28.2 billion in 2002. But farm income dropped by 24 per cent, and farm debt for fertilizer and other inputs doubled. Farmers always get the wrong end of the stick in an export economy, said Qualman, because they compete for sales with goods grown by a billion farmers, while everything they buy comes from three or four monopolies. 'The farm income crunch is caused by this imbalance of market power in the global food chain,' he says, which will work the same way for Africa's chocolate, cotton and coffee producers. The issue for Africa, Qualman said, was 'the right to build barriers, not tear them down'.

Annie Sugrue, who headed the South African community economic development group, Eco City, scoffed at the idea that trade would benefit a population where 46 per cent of the people survive on less than a dollar a day. 'It's complete rubbish to say they're going to be involved in trade,' she says. All of South Africa's clothing workers lost their jobs to imports from China, she adds. 'If anyone wants to help Africa, they should cancel trade, not just the debt.' European trade barriers to African food exports actually help the poor in Africa, she says, because they force local farmers to grow food for the local market instead of flowers for Europe.

Research from the UN Food and Agriculture Organization (FAO) confirms Qualman's and Sugrue's scorn for trade-based food strategies. The FAO's 2004 report documents that Southerners are exploited by powerful transnational monopolies. If export prices had stayed stable since 1980, countries in the Global South would have earned an additional $112 billion in 2002, more than double the amount received in foreign aid. What happened to the $112 billion? 'At the international level, a few vertically integrated companies have gained increasing control over agricultural trade,' and get the lion's share of money spent by Northern consumers, the report noted. 'Even with bananas, which require almost no processing, international trading companies, distributors and retailers claim 88 per cent of the retail price,' while 'barely two per cent' goes to plantation workers, the FAO reported. Yet, one year later, an FAO study promoted trade as the way out of poverty. The FAO campaigns regularly for free trade, cuts in subsidies for Northern farmers, and phasing out regulations that make it hard for processed foods from the Global South to enter Northern markets.[8]

Assembling food in China

If food exports and free trade offered a way out of poverty, China should be a shining example. It has the population base for mass production. It has diplomatic clout. It has a literate and disciplined workforce. China's shrewd food exporters know where they fit into the Western food system. After four decades of cheap food, Westerners don't buy food any more; they buy processed meals assembled from ingredients or 'inputs'. And that's where China comes in.

The strategy is to bundle, rather than grow or make. China has moved to control as many inputs as possible, and has become the dominant player in such items as Vitamin B and C, garlic, apples, apple juice, farmed fish, processed fish, honey, onions and organic broccoli.[9]

China offers low wages, low environmental standards and high labor discipline that the Global North can't match. When products require precision hand labor at low wages, Chinese exporters do it. For example, they do salmon, which have 36 pin bones best handled by hand, and crab, best removed by hand with pincers. No-one costs out the pollution from shipping and refrigerating salmon and crab from the North American west coast to China and then back. And few stop to ask who gets hurt most in this world of wage-based competition that is supposed to lead the way out of poverty.

The high cost of cheap food

Here's how one downward spiral unravels. China's cheap apples and apple juice beat out once-prized apples from western North America in North American markets; unsold apples from western North America are then dumped in India, bankrupting Indian apple producers. The world's farmers are turned into competitors with each other, transporting goods, mostly composed of water, back and forth around the world – transactions that are high in energy use but low in added value to health or social well-being. As for the impact of this export strategy in China, a 2006 report from China's National Development and Reform Commission documented stark inequalities. China's inequality between city and country 'would make many a modern capitalist blush', *The Economist* comments in an article on the report. The share of Gross Domestic Product (GDP) going to wages in China declined from 53 to 41 per cent during the period when exports exploded, from 1998 to 2005. Even when food exports are pursued by a powerful state following a shrewd strategy, China's experience shows that the relentless downward pressures of the global cheap food system prevail.[10]

Korean food routes and roots

South Korea is a different case study. Korea is one of the 'Asian Tigers' – Hong Kong, Taiwan and Singapore are others – a small group that that broke free of colonialism to become hubs of sophisticated industries and therefore a success story. The tiny peninsula is a star performer in many areas, including its healthy diet, featuring spicy *kimchi*, considered one of the world's superfoods. Though classified as undeveloped as recently as the 1950s, it is now one of the top 10 industrial powers in the world. Analysts of Korea's achievements give credit to an active state that planned industrial clusters strategically and invested heavily in education and social equality, factors usually left to look after themselves in typical promotions of export-led growth.

Despite urban and industrial successes, Korea's three-and-a-half million farmers are deeply troubled. Their pain was brought to world attention in 2003 when Lee Kyang Hae, a leading spokesperson for Korean farmers, chose the day of Korea's harvest celebration to stab himself to death outside a meeting of the World Trade Organization in Cancún, Mexico. About a hundred of his Korean friends sat down by his side and raised a banner in his honor: 'WTO Kills', a reference to the desperate situation of farmers forced to compete in their own home market against highly subsidized exports from the US and Europe.[11]

I was invited to South Korea to speak on local routes to food security in October 2006, just after North Korea tested its new nuclear weaponry. Environmental groups in South Korea were equally worried that food security and rural sustainability would blow up if a proposed bilateral free trade deal with the US was adopted, providing full frontal exposure to US cheap food. After the conference, Denise, a local organizer, takes me to meet members of a farm organization in a tiny mountain village called Deok-bong-san, about an hour by train from Seoul. We stroll up the hill to the village restaurant and meet She-ik Oh, introduced to me by Denise as a member of the local farmers' organization. He bows to me, and flashes a grin at Denise. 'I am a peasant, not a farmer,' he says to her in Korean. 'Farmers work for money. Peasants work because they love the land and are tied to it.' Who could ask for a better introduction?

We leave our shoes at the restaurant door and I meet several executive members of the local peasants' and farmers' league. After a few minutes of chatting, the president of the local league asks how old I am. That's a weird question to ask so soon, I say to myself before giving the answer. A bottle of 'farmers' wine' – a milk-like potion that farmers enjoy at lunch, claiming it gives them extra energy – is set on the table. Everyone pours a drink for someone else, never for themselves.

The high cost of cheap food

A nice touch of togetherness, I think. Then I notice that the person pouring my drink uses two hands instead of one, a mark of respect for the oldest person at the table. Respect for culture, tradition and community engulf Korean meals.

Far from being obsolete, Korean dishes may become the model for eco-superfoods of the coming century. Almost every serving embodies high-nutrient, low-calorie goodness, which may explain why I never saw one obese person during a nine-day tour of Korea's cities and countryside. Most dishes also express a food system that is as close to nature as it is to culture. At the center of the table, which everyone can reach with chopsticks, there's a bowl of pork, commonly raised on food scraps rather than grains, and several dishes of fish, shellfish and seaweed from the ocean, an hour's drive away. About ten veggie dishes are passed around – tofu, sweet potato, cucumber (grown by my peasant friend, She-ik), mushrooms, several varieties of *kimchi* (cabbage fermented with ginger, red chili pepper and garlic), lettuce, collards, and carrots. A range of green leaves are used as low-calorie wraps in place of bread. Many dishes use parts of a plant that would be wasted in North America – leaves of squash used as wraps, or persimmon leaves used in tea, for example. Several dishes, such as miso and kimchi, are fermented, a low-tech and low-energy form of preservation that adds healthy enzymes to food.

Korea's special national foods are eaten daily, not just on rare holidays. These identity foods evolved from a frugal folk culture based on local ingredients cooked at home from scratch. Though Korea is ultra-modern in its technology, education, clothing, entertainments and politics, food still expresses tradition that predates mechanization, long-haul transportation, processing, packaging, microwaving of prepared foods and eating alone. Meat is not the center of the meal. Rice is. We each have our own silver bowl, and Denise discreetly elbows me to make sure I finish mine and sing its praises. Rice is a specialty of the area, in a country where rice is a sacramental staple filling people with identity, spirituality and culture. It is used in rice wine, rice cakes and an after-dinner drink of sweet rice water left after the cooking, as well as eaten in its own bowl at every meal.

After lunch, we stroll up to the home of the wealthiest farmer in the village, who raises more than 20 cows for meat. (They don't raise steers as in North America and Europe, since cows provide both meat and offspring.) We sip pine-leaf tea fermented in honey. The pines and the mountain ranges they cover are symbols of permanence, disturbed only by a few Buddhist temples, rarely by monster homes. Like many iconic Korean foods – ginseng and green tea are best known – pine tea and honey are foraged from the mountains that occupy two-thirds of the landscape. Korean food has the taste of Korea's sea, land and mountains.

A brief tour of farms along the valley reveals many farms of only a few hectares, most of which make full use of space by growing vegetables in low-tech greenhouses. Rice farms are mostly about 10 hectares. I watch the rice being harvested by a small crew with a combine, leased by day from the local government, a shrewd way to keep capital costs down in a small operation. To save farm space, the rice is dried on canvas by the side of the country road. Despite rich soil, hard work, deep knowledge and careful use of resources, everyone I speak with expresses sadness that their children never think of taking up a poorly paid future in farming. Everyone blames their plight on cheap imports from the US, one of the world's leading rice exporters, and shudders with fear as to their future now that the free trade deal with the US is in place.

More such trade deals are likely in Asia's future. Anyone who's tracked the tobacco industry knows how it shifted its sights to Asia as soon as health alarms went off in Europe and North America during the 1960s. The same survival strategy for obsolete industries applies to junk food, which also needs fresh and unprepared markets to conquer. Free trade deals allow in cheap carbs and meat from afar, damaging fragile folk systems of eating, engaging with food and living.

The hidden cost of cheap food

How can the damage that a cheap food system does to traditional cultures be calculated in dollar terms? Indeed, cheap food is actually anything but cheap. The sticker price at the store may be low. The percentage of income going to food may be low. The full, or lifecycle, cost of cheap food, however, 'from grow it to throw it', is another matter. Cheap food is an elaborate 'buy now, pay later' sales scheme. After paying a bargain price at the cash register come several charges that no-one bargained for. The paradox of expensive cheap food comes from hidden costs that most people don't see or anticipate. Besides the incalculable impact on world cultures, there are five other kinds of these hidden costs, which are worth reviewing to get a sense of the size of the pot of money that is now wasted on hidden costs, but could be used in a more creative way.

1 Poor health

The first hidden cost flows from the principle that 'what goes around comes around'. Cheap food gets people coming and going. There's a low-priced aisle in the supermarket for foods that have had fiber removed, and a high-priced aisle for laxatives, antacids and upset tummy remedies. Junk costs as much to get rid of as to buy. British taxpayers pay $85 million a year to cover laxatives for seniors, a fraction of the cost paid by all those suffering from constipation. These expenses can be avoided by eating fiber-rich unprocessed food. Constipation reveals a food system that's stuck because it's only cheap and easy at the front end. The fact that one third of all cancers are linked to poor diet reveals the longer-term consequences. Since the additional expense is charged to health rather than agricultural expenditure, the hidden subsidy to cheap food isn't visible.[12]

2 Poverty

The second hidden cost of cheap food comes from the inevitable and expensive poverty, inequality and disruption that come from underpaying farmers and food workers. Since government programs to cope with the consequences of poverty are classified as social development or welfare, few people connect the dots to the cheap food system. The rise of cheap food since the 1970s coincides with rising inequality throughout the world, including in relatively affluent countries where McJobs have displaced jobs that once paid a living wage. In the Global South, cheap food leads to two troubling migration trends of the last decades. First is the exodus of poor people from rural areas, what *Planet of Slums* author Mike Davis calls the 'mass production of slums' – a trend enveloping about 40 per cent of the people of the Global South. This trend depopulates one area to overpopulate another, forcing people to leave an area where costs of living are relatively low to seek work in an area where costs of land, housing and food are high.

The second migration trend turns the young and restless poor into nomads without a country. Until recently, most short-term migration for temporary farm jobs was to the Global North. It's now estimated that over 70 million 'South to South' migrants are in transit, looking for seasonal farm work in another low-waged country of the Global South. Since the 1990s in Nicaragua, for example, some 500,000 people a year have been traveling throughout Central America to find seasonal farm jobs, a process that disrupts their personal, family and village life. Nicaraguan economist Francisco Mayorga describes the trend as a new form of pillaging the colonial world. The trend, argues sociologist Philip

McMichael, is no longer 'simply about producing cheap food'. Since cheap food imposes disorganization on the entire structure of economies and societies, 'it is also about securing new conditions for accumulation by lowering the cost of labor worldwide,' he argues.[13]

3 Environmental damage

The third hidden cost of cheap food comes from repairing damage to the environment after producers 'externalize' the costs of proper stewardship thanks to what's called a 'regulatory subsidy'. When producers 'externalize' a cost, they get rid of a problem they cause – by polluting a waterway with pesticide run-off, for example. When governments allow farmers and companies to cut their costs in this way, it's a regulatory subsidy. In effect it's a hidden subsidy, since no formal grants are required, just turning blind eyes.

Conventional agriculture contributes to soil erosion and pollution of land, water and air. Some clean-up is required before people drink the water and breathe the air. So taxpayers end up paying the cleaning bill after the regulatory subsidy. British farm analyst Jules Pretty worked up some estimates for a few clean-up costs and concluded that British taxpayers spend $45-$50 to clean up water damage passed on by every hectare of farmland.[14]

4 Food waste

When something is priced too cheap, it is often wasted. And so it is with food in the Global North. Wasted food is not only a benefit lost. It is harm done, as when tossed food ends up in landfill, and where rot turns into methane, with 22 times more global-warming effect than carbon dioxide – methane which can almost effortlessly be harvested from landfills as a clean-burning fuel akin to natural gas. Also in the Global North, perfectly good but undervalued foods and food byproducts are wasted that could more easily provide positive functions and address global-warming reduction targets. Every municipality could convert its waste-management department into a resource-recovery department.

Much can be gleaned from Vaclav Smil, leading geographer and author of *Feeding the World: A Challenge for the Twenty-First Century*. 'Our response to higher demand should not be primarily the quest for higher supply through increased inputs, but rather the pursuit of higher efficiency,' he writes. 'Higher conversion efficiencies are our best prevention and defense' against shortages. Smil is concerned by the fixation he sees with improving farmer or fisher productivity, with millions of dollars spent to jack up production by one per cent. Yet he sees no attention to increasing productivity of waste – or rather, resource – management.

A little care in post-harvest handling could end the wasting of 10 per cent of cereals, more than 25 per cent of spoiled fruits and vegetables – and even more fishery 'bycatch', valuable fish tossed overboard because the crew isn't paid to bring them back. 'We should look for more food not only in fields, pastures, barns and ponds but also in storage bins and sheds, in warehouses and supermarkets, in food service and in household pantries and refrigerators,' Smil argues. Despite all the institutions fretting about increased production, he notes, 'We do not have even a single organization devoted to the worldwide problem of food losses.'

Smil estimates that the energy and nutrient equivalent of 100 megatonnes of grain a year, 'nearly half of all cereals on the world market', could be conserved if the 'rich world' reduced its overall waste by 20 per cent. In my experience, that would be a snap. When I and my family do a stint of volunteering on organic farms each summer, we usually spend the hottest hour of the day culling the items that can't be sold. Nothing is wrong with these items from the standpoint of safety, nutrition or taste. They just don't look the way they do in the food magazines. The carrots are misshapen, the broccoli heads are a little small and the apples have a few scabs – they are all cosmetically challenged. About a third of the fruits and vegetables grown in North America don't get to the store, and may never even be harvested, because of this. Similar culls take place at processors and supermarkets. A screw-up in labeling or packaging ends up as garbage. When dairy products get close to their best-before dates, the milk is tossed. No customer wants to buy milk on 5 June that may go off on 7 June, and no retailer wants to keep the brand-new shipment of milk in storage until the old stuff has sold. Home waste is at least as bad. Standard estimates for consumer wastage in the Global North are in the 25-to-40 per cent range.[15]

Food banks in the Global North try to reclaim a small portion of packaged items with long shelf life to donate as charity for the poor. Linking waste management to poverty alleviation is the low end of food conservation. Food banks would be doing the world a much bigger favor, Mark Winne has argued in *Closing the Food Gap*, by campaigning for adequate incomes to make safe, nutritious food affordable and to promote personal and community self-help projects such as community gardens and community kitchens.[16]

5 Food adulteration

The fifth hidden cost of cheap food is harder to calculate financially. Many of the methods used to keep sticker prices down insult taste buds as well as health, as when jams are filled with more sugar than fruit, or 'plump' chickens are pumped up with water, or yeasty breads become vehicles to supplement flour with free air. Chicken should be sold by the liter, not the pound, one critic told me. The universal presence of salt, sugar and corn – usually labeled according to the chemical property they provide rather than the product most people can recognize – testifies to the extent of product substitution in low-cost foods. If the label requires an advanced science degree to understand, the likelihood is that chemicals are standing in for real ingredients with more complex tastes.

Market failure

Cheap food has prevailed for some time because of 'market failure' compounded by political failures. Market failure refers to a 'collective action problem' that keeps sellers and buyers from co-operating to solve common problems that need to be solved. When everyone has to stand up at an outdoor concert because a few people at the front won't sit down, that's a lose-lose situation that comes from collective action problems in crowds. The hidden costs of cheap food indicate lose-lose situations that collective action needs to correct because market forces haven't been able to do so.[17]

Until recently, moving to correct market failure in the food and agriculture sector wasn't rocket science. Governments have long regulated food safety, for example. Likewise, there are longstanding government programs to encourage farm research and education. There also used to be programs to prevent food prices from falling so low that they threatened future food security and environmental quality. The original modernists favored many of them. From 1947 to 1993, the General Agreement on Tariffs and Trade (GATT) permitted governments to assist and protect domestic farmers to protect their market share and ensure that they could produce food into the future. The rush to deregulate food policy after the World Trade Organization displaced GATT in 1995 trumped centuries of experience with food as a foundation stone of health, culture, community and the economy – relationships that couldn't be entirely trusted to the blind forces of the market.[18]

Experience before and since 1995 confirms that market forces need public help to correct the cheap food spiral. The very nature of food and farming, not just the greed of individuals or corporations, predetermines that self-regulation can't solve this problem. To start with, food goes bad quickly. No-one wants sour milk or rotting fruit. So farmers start losing bargaining power every hour after the food is ready, especially at harvest time when all the farmers in an area have food they need to move fast. Few industries deal with such relentless pressures to sell fast at any price. Second, farmers with expensive land or equipment face pressures to take any price that pays off the loans so their farms don't get seized. So, when prices go down, farmers with big expensive tractors produce more, which makes prices fall even lower. Far from an investment in future rewards or food security for the population, investment in farm equipment turns farmers into price takers, not price makers.

Agricultural subsidies – producer support as % of gross farm receipts

	2004	2005	2006	2007	2008	2009	2010	2011
Australia	3	4	5	5	4	3	3	3
Canada	20	21	21	16	13	17	17	14
Chile	5	5	4	4	3	6	3	4
Iceland	66	67	64	56	52	51	47	44
Japan	56	54	52	47	48	49	53	52
Korea	61	60	59	57	46	51	45	53
Mexico	12	13	13	13	12	14	12	12
New Zealand	1	1	1	1	1	0	1	1
Norway	66	66	64	55	59	61	61	58
Switzerland	69	66	65	49	56	60	54	54
Turkey	32	33	33	26	26	28	26	20
United States	16	15	11	10	9	11	8	8
EU27	33	30	29	23	22	23	20	18
OECD- Total	30	29	26	22	21	23	20	19

Last updated: 28 January 2013; disclaimer: http://oe.cd/disclaimer

Source: Producer and Consumer Support Estimates: Producer support estimate and related indicators by country, OECD Agriculture Statistics

Third, controlling supply is as hard as controlling climate, not as easy as shutting down an assembly line. Perennial crops such as apples and grapes keep on coming, no matter what the price. Nor do cows stop giving milk, or hens stop laying eggs in response to market signals. Even seemingly all-powerful corporations face these relentless pressures. Food shoppers don't look, then come back a week later and buy. In the food business, a missed sale is lost forever. Despite high levels of ownership concentration in the food industry, price wars are more common than co-operation or collusion to limit the cutthroat discounting that's cannibalizing many sectors of the food industry.

University of Tennessee farm economist Daryll Ray has exposed the nooks and crannies of market failure in the food sector for over a decade. A 30-year wave of farm bankruptcies in the US, the global price leader in the food industry, 'is the direct result of expanding productive capacity while ignoring the need for policies to manage the use of that capacity,' Ray argues. Unwilling to manage supply – that would be intervening in the marketplace – the US government dishes out subsidies to cover farm losses, which is apparently not intervening in the marketplace. Many governments in affluent countries follow suit, which accounts for $280 billion a year in farm subsidies spent in major industrial countries.[19]

The high sticker price of cheap food

But the most recent and startling game-changer for cheap food is that the sticker price is now rising as fast as the hidden price. After 40 years of costs declining at the rate of 0.6 per cent a year, costs started rising in the new millennium. By 2010, global food prices had doubled. In the Global North, the rise in food prices has been masked because the raw ingredients are a relatively minor portion of the cost of processed or prepared foods. But for the two billion people in the Global

The high cost of cheap food

South who live on less than two dollars a day and rely on staples, it was catastrophic, leading to widespread rioting in 40 countries in 2008 and protests feeding into the Arab Spring of 2010.[20]

Increased prices for food, conventional reasoning goes, respond to either reduced supplies of food or increased demands for food – it's the law of supply and demand that's at work, nothing more or less. Such an analysis doesn't take the food system into account as a molder of both supply and demand. My explanation lists three sets of factors – supply, demand and food system.

Powerful forces have increased the demand for food and for non-food uses to which food can be put. Most obvious as a demand factor is the increase in world population, from 6 billion in 1999 to 7 billion in 2012. This effect was amplified in 2008, the first time when fully half the people in the world lived in cities. More people than ever before ate food without producing it. These demographic facts increased demand considerably.

No new supplies of food came on stream in this period. Rapid population growth after the 1960s had minimal impact on food prices because new methods of raising food were increasing yields, and because farmers converted 434 million hectares from wilderness to agriculture.

What could be simpler or more predetermined? The formula says: demand is up, supply is steady, and so prices go up. But the modernist food system that rose to global dominance after World War Two has its own impacts on both supply and demand.

As a system based on industrial principles, for example, it designs for simplification and standardization. The fewer the variations on an assembly line, the better. Survival of the fittest for industrial food organization meant that an estimated 75 per cent of the world's agricultural varieties have been lost or forgotten since the 1950s. Only about 150 of at least 7,500 edible species are raised commercially. A dozen plants account for 80 per cent of the calories people eat – corn (maize), rice, wheat, soybeans, potatoes, bananas, plantain, sorghum, cassava, millet, sunflowers and canola. Three crops – corn, wheat and rice – account for 40 per cent of human calories. Since most corn, for example, is fed to livestock, a 20-per-cent increase in demand for meat – in part created by rising middle classes in India and China – has an enormous impact on the demand for and price of grains destined for two billion of the world's most vulnerable people. The fact that they must compete with livestock for grains is the result of the food system, not just laws of supply and demand. In addition, one third of the US corn crop is being converted to ethanol, an alcohol-based fuel. The only law of supply and demand at work here is the farm subsidy laws that pay for an over-supply of corn, and a 500-per-cent increase in ethanol from corn and sugar between 2000 and 2011. The high price for corn is strictly a case of manufactured scarcity, courtesy of an industrial food system.[21] Were it not for government subsidies, farmers would respond to market signals and switch to production of healthier, more environmentally friendly foods.

A food system presenting itself as offering unprecedented choice has ratcheted down real choice and turned the likes of buckwheat, barley, rye, oats, quinoa, amaranth, teff, lentils, chickpea, peppers, tomatoes, bok choy, eggplant and carrots into specialty crops. A food system built on such a limited and vulnerable foundation is asking for trouble – from weather that's not perfect, from pest levels that change from year to year, or from speculators out to corner the market.[22]

The seemingly impossible trick of cheap food after the 1970s was to keep prices down while upping the amount of normally expensive meat, energy, packaging and convenience in daily meals. It's hard to do that without killing the goose that lays the golden eggs. This is what happened with overfishing, for example. Industrial fleets that mined the ocean for fish made short work of many stocks, most famously the limitless cod that once jumped into the baskets of European fishers off the coast of Newfoundland. It's estimated that 75 per cent of major marine fish stocks are either over-exploited or fished to their limit.[23] Likewise, reduced grain harvests in many parts of the world since 2007 have been attributed to the impacts of soil degradation, high temperatures and drought. These conditions are all aggravated by farming methods that sacrifice long-term stewardship of the land to short-term gains.[24]

The rise of speculation

The impact of speculators on food prices after 2007, now confirmed by economic studies, is also an indication of a food system gone haywire, not the workings of laws of supply and demand. For the same reason that poker players with a good hand still hedge their bets, farmers have long hedged their bets on crops, rather than risk losing everything in the event of a summer storm or swarm of pests. A farmer accepts a given price from a trader early in the season, and is guaranteed to end the season with something. This practice mimicked the real level of guesswork in the real world.[25]

By contrast, today's speculation started in 1981, when five investment firms, including Goldman Sachs, bought into commodity trading firms. A decade later, Goldman Sachs developed a commodities index that included wheat, corn and soybeans. In 2000, the US government passed a law making this previously banned practice legal, thereby allowing Wall Street-based investors and traders into a scene that once served farmers, not bankers. Once the proverbial fox got into the henhouse, power over pricing shifted to the most powerful and wily financial wizards of a world economy, with little knowledge of or concern for the intricacies of crops that billions of people depended on to stay alive.

Food had always been treated as a commodity with a social purpose in the post-War modernist world.

But, as of 1991, food was listed on the stock market and treated exclusively as a commodity. Moreover, in 1996, the US government ended the practice, which went back generations, of holding reserves of harvests from good years in the event a bad year came along. Without reserves to maintain stability during a rocky year, speculation could run amok – which it did in 2007 and 2008. The most sophisticated economic analysis of the price hikes at that time fingers the signal roles of both ethanol and speculation. By integrating short-term investors and speculators in the food system, the US government put the cheap food system under the control of a financial sector that only wins when prices go up.[26]

1 S Mintz, *Sweetness and Power*, Penguin, 1986. **2** P McMichael, *Development and Social Change: A Global Perspective*, Pine Forge Press, 2000. **3** P McMichael, 'Global Food Politics', in *Monthly Review,* Vol 50 No 3 Jul-Aug 1998; FAO, *The State of Food and Agriculture*, 2005, p 172. **4** T Winson, *The Intimate Commodity*, Garamond Press, 1995; M Vander Stichele and S van der Wal, *The Profit Behind Your Plate*, SOMO, 2006, pp 13, 15, 33; Debbie Barker, *The Rise and Predictable Fall of Globalized Industrial Agriculture*, International Forum on Globalization, 2007, p 7; H Schaffer et al, 'US Agricultural Commodity Policy and its Relationship to Obesity', background paper developed for the Wingspread Conference, Mar 2007. **5** J Kolko, *Restructuring the World Economy*, Pantheon, 1988. **6** G Albo, 'Competitive Austerity and the Impasse of Capitalist Employment Policy', in R Miliband and L Panitch, *Socialist Register* 30 (Merlin Press,1994); G Albo, 'A World Market of Opportunities? Capitalist Obstacles and Left Economic Policy,' in L Panitch, ed, *Socialist Register 33* (Merlin Press, 1997). **7** FAO, *The State of Agricultural Commodity Markets*, 2004, pp 41-3. **8** FAO, *The State of Agricultural Commodity Markets 2004*, especially pp 14, 31; FAO, *The State of Food and Agriculture 2005*; OECD, *Agricultural Trade and Poverty*, 2003. **9** 'Economics Focus, An old Chinese myth', in *The Economist*, 5 Jan 2008, p 75; 'How Fit is the Panda?,' *The Economist*, 29 Sep 2007; 'The great unbundling', *The Economist*, 20 Jan 2007. For daily coverage of Chinese food safety practices, go to www.foodsafetynetwork.ca archives, and search 'China.' **10** G York, 'China frets over widening income disparity' in *Globe and Mail*, 9 Feb 2006, pp 1, 18; *The Economist*, 13 Oct 2007, pp 15, 90. **11** D Rodrik, 'Getting Interventions Right', in *National Bureau of Economic Research*, Working Paper 4964, 1994; R Wade, *Growing the Market*, Princeton University Press, 2003. **12** M. Petticrew et al, 'Systematic review of the effectiveness of laxatives in the elderly', in *Health Technology Assessment*, Vol 1, No 13, 1997. **13** See nin. tl/14beSNn; P McMichael 'Book Review: The End of Poverty: Possibilities for Our Time', in *International Journal of Comparative Sociology*, Vol 46, No

The high cost of cheap food

4, 2005 ; P McMichael, 'Peasants make their own history, but not as they please', *Journal of Agrarian Change* 8, 1990, pp 205-228. **14** J Pretty, *The Living Land*, Earthscan, 2001, p 78. **15** For sample reports on waste, see: nin.tl/YOfBmA ; L Heller and J Luesby, 'Arizona study finds we waste half of food we produce,' *Agribusiness Examiner*, 16 Aug 2005; Organic Consumers Association, 'US Wastes \$14 bill in Food and Crops Every Year,' 20 Jun 2005, nin.tl/14bg6YZ; *Sustainability Planning News*, 18 Mar 2007; 'Britain Wastes as Much as Half the Food it Produces', terradaily, 3 Mar 2008. **16** M Winne, *Closing the Food Gap*, Beacon Press, 2008. **17** C Rocha, 'Food Insecurity as Market Failure', in *Journal of Hunger and Environmental Nutrition*, Vol 1, No 4, 2007. **18** EC Pasour, 'Intellectual Tyranny of the Status Quo', Econ Journal Watch, Vol 1, No 1, Apr 2004; M Pollan, *In Defense of Food*, Penguin, 2008. **19** D Ray et al, *Rethinking US Agricultural Policy*, Agricultural Policy Analysis Center, University of Tennessee, 2003; D Ray, 'A New Vision for Agricultural Policy', Presentation to the National Family Farm Coalition, Washington DC, 30 Jan 2005; H Schaffer et al, 'US Agricultural Commodity Policy and its Relationship to Obesity', background paper developed for the Wingspread Conference, Mar 2007. **20** S Wenzlau, 'Global Food Prices Continue to Rise,' *Nourishing the Planet*, 11 Apr, 2013; L Brown, 'Full Planet, Empty Plates,' at www.earthpolicy.org **21** 'Global Meat Production and Consumption Continue to Rise,' Worldwatch Institute, 13 May 2013; 'Global Meat Consumption', *The Globalist*, 23 Apr 2013. **22** FAO, *State of the World's Plant Genetic Resources for Food and Agriculture*, Rome, 1997; EO Wilson, *The Diversity of Life*, Harvard University Press, 1992. **23** nin.tl/YOgHyF **24** On supply-side shortages, see 'China yearly shortfalls in wheat ...' AP-Foodtechnology.com 8 Oct 2007; 'Global Production Shortfalls Bring record Wheat Prices', in *Amber Waves*, Nov 2007; J von Braun, *The World Food Situation*, International Food Policy Research Institute, Dec 2007; 'Development: Food Prices Climbing With No End in Sight', Inter Press Service, 5 Dec 2007; Reuters, 19 Mar 2007, posted in Rachel's Democracy and Health News, 899, 22 Mar 2007; 'Australia drought hit world's third largest wheat exporter and key supplier...,' *San Jose Mercury News*, 16 Mar 2007; 'The big dry,' *The Economist*, 28 Apr 2007, pp 81-2. **25** M.Lagi et al, 'The Food Crises', New England Complex Systems Institute, 23 Sep 2011; S Murphy et al, *Cereal Secrets*, Oxfam Research reports, Aug 2012. **26** R Patel, 'The Long Green Revolution,' *The Journal of Peasant Studies*, 40:1 2013, pp 35-6; J Clapp, *Food*, (Polity Press, 2012).

4 A tale of two worlds: understanding food sovereignty

Food sovereignty is a powerful but challenging understanding of food rights that came onto the world scene during the 1990s, as part of a peasant-led campaign against the World Trade Organization. This chapter argues that food sovereignty ideals grew out of a deeply social and spiritual food culture in the Global South. Both the agricultural practices and community food culture behind food sovereignty challenge the more Northern notion of food security.

PEOPLE ACTIVE in food organizations have a hard time giving 'elevator speeches' – explanations of what they stand for that can be said and understood in the time it takes to ride an elevator. Two food terms befuddle most people, including food advocates and experts. Food security is one. Food sovereignty is the other. It takes longer to read this chapter than to ride an elevator, but I will try to explain what the two terms mean, how they relate, and where they come from.

Whoever coined the two terms probably thought they were being helpful by coupling food, a word that everyone understands, needs and thinks well of, with another word – either security or sovereignty – people also recognize and have positive thoughts about.

Food security, for example, builds on a well-established understanding of national security, which refers to the right of a country to control the key factors affecting the safety and well-being of its citizens. Equally powerful and longstanding notions of individualism sit well with notions of national security because there's an understanding that individual rights are nested in the larger community, and both need to be protected together. Some people are old enough to remember when governments sponsored social security and income security programs, and when unions were able to defend job security – all ways in which collective and individual security could be paired. That's the sense food security advocates at the United Nations evoke when they latch food onto security. The formal definition of food security is that all people at all times have access to adequate amounts of safe, nutritious and culturally appropriate food. It expresses both an individual and community right. The UN has been using the term since the mid-1970s, when world food prices were going through the roof as a result of skyrocketing oil prices, and the US government, led by Secretary of State Henry Kissinger, orchestrated international gatherings to respond to the world food crisis.

More recently, security has been given a spin related to security guards who protect against outside threats – be they thieves or terrorists. As a result of this twist to the notion of security, many people think food security is about protecting the food supply from contamination by bio-terrorists or avian flu. The emphasis on external threats in this understanding of food security distorts understanding of food issues considerably, because there are doubtless more poisons entering the food system and water supply via farm pesticides than via deliberate murder plots, and because the outside threat distracts attention from internal threats, such as hunger and obesity. Nevertheless, I got a kick out of the way this fearful spin on food security worked to my advantage, because I always had an easy time crossing the border into the US for board meetings of the Community Food Security Coalition. Godspeed, the guards would immediately say, when I said I worked with Toronto Public Health and was off to a food security meeting.

Little did the border guards know that the Coalition chose its name to challenge the US government's effort during the 1990s to de-emphasize the community connection by referring to the rising problem of hunger in low-income communities as a 'household food security' issue. This implied that only individual households, not broader communities, have a problem with and responsibility for food security, thereby legitimizing private charity as the way to respond to an individual problem – a nice reminder of how words can 'frame' issues without anyone being aware of it. In 1994, when a group of North American food justice advocates wanted to work together and were casting about for a name, Mark Winne from the Hartford Food System in Connecticut suggested 'community food security', because it countered US government efforts to individualize the term. The Community Food Security Coalition was so named. In my opinion, his wonderful muddying of the waters brings community food security to within a hair's breadth of meaning the same thing as food sovereignty.

The impact of the World Trade Organization

'North is north and south is south, and never the twain shall meet' applies to developments that gave rise to food sovereignty thinking in the Global South during the 1990s, and which took many in the Global North by surprise.

The 1990s are largely identified with the rise of what's called neoliberalism, which got a boost when the Soviet Union collapsed in 1989, widely taken to prove that state control of economies was a bad thing for both personal liberty and economic prosperity. Neoliberals, in theory, believe a state has no business meddling with either the private behavior of individuals or the economic behavior of private corporations. Unlike their namesakes, the kind of liberals who supported 'mixed economies' after World War Two, the next-generation neoliberals thought governments should vacate the private sector and leave businesses and their employees to fend for themselves in an economy driven by the market. Neoliberal ideologues, backed by many leaders of global corporations, saw free trade deals as vehicles to embed rules limiting government powers to intervene in the economy.

The high water mark of neoliberal success came with the birth of the World Trade Organization (WTO) in 1995. Until the formation of the WTO, world trade bodies seldom interfered with the food and agriculture policies of any country, because food was considered a national security issue for which all governments needed to plan, and because food was such a central factor in the employment and health policies of all countries. As a result, the leading world body since the 1940s, called the General Agreement on Tariffs and Trade (GATT), exempted food and agriculture from its efforts to promote freer trade. The WTO succeeded GATT, and upended its old approach by prohibiting laws or programs protecting local farming, fishing or food interests from foreign competitors or investors. In effect, the WTO defined food matters as a simple business proposition like any other, which should live or die in the marketplace. This reversed an important element of the global food system that emerged after World War Two. But in 1995, it officially became the defining element.

The WTO changed just about everything in the world, largely because it trumped all other international agreements, such as agreements on the rights of children, workers, women and so on. But the WTO did not have an identical impact on everyone. For example, it affected the Global North and Global South quite differently. In the Global North, globalization was most painfully linked with the outsourcing of well-paying industrial jobs to the Global South. Blue-collar workers, especially in what came to be called 'rustbelt towns', were the major economic losers. Consumers, including laid-off industrial workers, benefited from the onrush of cheap foods, clothes and household items imported from the Global South. The era of government programs that either protected the economic needs of vulnerable people or protected the universal economic, health or environmental needs of all citizens – the norm for Northern governments of all political stripes during the 1940s, 1950s and 1960s – pretty well came to an end. To date, however, the traumatizing impact of globalization on previously well-organized industrial working-class and middle-income individuals and communities has not sparked anything like a unified international movement united behind a movement for 'industrial sovereignty'. Nor have farmers of the Global North identified globalization as a major force responsible for their woes, since many still hope to win the competition. The main groups supporting local foods against globalization in the Global North are urban food enthusiasts, not blue-collar workers or farmers, who find most local products simply too expensive.

The picture is reversed in the Global South, where globalization has meant more jobs for blue-collar workers. In this bizarre version of musical chairs, imports of cheap foods subsidized by Global North taxpayers provide a lower-cost diet for Global South factory workers. The Global South factory owners recruit workers who are streaming into the swelling cities from the countryside because they see no future in food production when markets are swamped by cheap food imports from the North. To understand why the smallest subsidy from the North has an enormous impact on the purchasing behavior of city workers in Asia, Africa or South America, it's worth remembering that people making less than two dollars a day in the Global South spend up to 40 per cent of their earnings on food staples, compared to North American and European workers who might spend between 10 and 20 of per cent of what they earn. Very marginal differences in the price of food can make a life-and-death difference to people in the Global South unless their governments do something forceful to support local production – which is what food sovereignty promotes.

A tale of two worlds

When WTO rules came into effect in the mid-1990s, farmers and peasants in the Global South were shell-shocked by the collapse of prices in their home markets – the net result of having to compete against heavily subsidized exports from Europe and the US, which basically set the world price for most food staples. For example, the relatively small but heavily subsidized US rice crop sets the world price for rice, since so few Asian countries have sufficient surplus to export. Consequently, even a relatively small increase in exported goods in an economy can have an enormous impact, especially when it ends up affecting people who usually earn less than two dollars a day.

Peasant protest

Organizations such as La Via Campesina (loosely translated, the Peasants' or Countrypeople's Way) quickly responded to the WTO rules and demanded 'Take Agriculture out of the WTO' – they wanted to restore some of the protections that farmers, farmworkers and peasants enjoyed before 1995. Founded in 1992, La Via Campesina represents some 200 million peasants, small farmers, agricultural workers and indigenous people from 70 countries. The organization developed and promoted the new concept of food sovereignty. This enhanced the concept of national independence of former colonies during the 1950s and 1960s, and repudiated consumer sovereignty as the sole dictating force of food prices and production practices.

Food sovereignty comes out of the mass impoverishment of peasants and fisherfolk in the Global South caused by World Trade Organization demands for sudden transitions to deregulation and free trade in food products. Peasant organizers throughout the Global South argued that trade rules prevailing before the 1990s, which exempted food and agriculture from free-trade deals, should be restored. That way, local food systems could be protected as foundation stones of the economy, community, culture and food security. Such autonomy was a cornerstone of food sovereignty. In 1996, La Via Campesina organizers took their point of view to a UN World Food Summit in Rome.

Why don't these campaigners limit their complaint to the subsidies that give the Global North's food exports such an unfair advantage in the markets? Why are their speeches so hostile to the WTO and to neoliberalism in general? Again, we need to recognize the very different realities in the Global South and the Global North.

In the Global North, neoliberals and WTO leaders are commonly referred to as champions of market forces, using free trade, privatization and deregulation as basic tools to cut back on government control over economies. This misrepresents reality. To understand the WTO and neoliberals, keep your eye on the ball, not your ear on the words. The WTO does not prevent the European Union or the US or any member of the

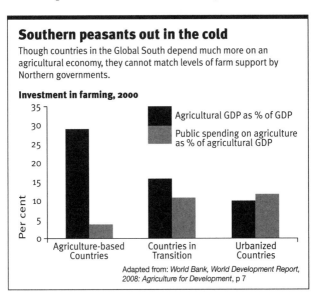

Southern peasants out in the cold

Though countries in the Global South depend much more on an agricultural economy, they cannot match levels of farm support by Northern governments.

Investment in farming, 2000

Legend:
- Agricultural GDP as % of GDP
- Public spending on agriculture as % of agricultural GDP

Y-axis: Per cent (0 to 35)

Categories: Agriculture-based Countries, Countries in Transition, Urbanized Countries

Adapted from: *World Bank, World Development Report, 2008: Agriculture for Development*, p 7

A tale of two worlds

BRICS nations (Brazil, Russia, India, China, South Africa) from protecting their farmers, fishers or global food corporations from foreign competition, or from subsidizing research promoting genetic engineering (GE), or from subsidizing food exports, or, as in 2008, from bailing out banks that would otherwise have gone bankrupt in a free-market economy. In short, there is not a shred of truth to the description of neoliberals or the WTO as supporters of the general principles of market forces, free trade, or privatization of anything much besides public utilities.

Indeed, food exporters and GE seed companies are as dependent on government payouts as munitions makers. Food companies needing protection in domestic markets rely on one regulation or another to keep out otherwise-competitive imports. US school meals, for example, baldly insist on US-sourced food. The more subtle Europeans impose food-safety regulations that Southern exporters can't meet. Food sovereignty can be understood as an effort by producers in the Global South to protect themselves from double standards such as these, not from international competition. What's good for the goose is good for the gander is one way to normalize understanding of food sovereignty. It's the same thinking that prevailed throughout the world before 1995, and the same practice that prevails in many places outside the Global South. To this extent, food sovereignty is not a radical or innovative idea, but a customary one.

Food sovereignty or food security?

Food sovereignty melds together two words that rarely ran into each other before.[1] Food and sovereignty paired well in the Global South for several reasons. First, countries of the Global South remain fundamentally rural countries. Peasants, farmworkers and fisherfolk are a majority of the population, unlike their counterparts in the Global North. Second, food producers do not self-define as a special-interest group or as a business, as they do in the Global North, where the concept of agribusiness has taken hold. Food producers are more likely to define themselves by the non-monetary values they hold and the practices they follow. As a result, the interests of peasants or farmers and the interests of the people in general are considered one and the same in the Global South. Third, many countries in the Global South have recently fought for and won national independence from European rulers. The pride and value of sovereignty are fresh in many people's memories, and inform a tradition around food campaigns.

I take this much space to explain the distinctive outlook of people from the Global South because I had to work through these issues myself back in 2002, when I attended my first international food conference – the World Food Summit in Rome. The whole scene was emotionally difficult for me, starting with a demonstration of citizen delegates the day before the Summit opened. This event came hard on the heels of the September 2001 terrorist attack in New York, and authorities in Rome had prepared for a confrontation. Young hostile-looking and armed soldiers lined the entire length of the avenue we marched along. Close to me, a young woman from South America broke into hysteria at the sight of these soldiers, and explained that she had been arrested, jailed and repeatedly raped by men looking just like them for having organized a peasant demonstration. I could only think of how easy I had it, paid by a city government to advocate for food security and to be away at a conference in Rome, and what incredible bravery it took to do the same work in other countries. For the next three days, with the exception of a five-minute period when almost everyone at the conference jumped out of their seats and ran out of the auditorium (I thought they were fed up with the conference, but people had just heard that a goal had been scored in a soccer game), NGO members from the

Global North were verbally hammered for their support of food security, rather than food sovereignty. That was the first time I realized that food security, a term I had been coming to like, was considered oppressive.

People like Peter Rosset of Food First and Pat Mooney of ETC Group talked me through the issues, however, and, before I knew it, I was the Canadian representative on the steering committee of the International Policy Committee coming out of the conference. That only lasted six months or so, but some intense meetings brought me up to speed on the background I needed. I reoriented my thinking, and am happy to help others do the same.

Food sovereignty comes from the protest of poor peasants and farmers who, among other things, faced bankruptcy as a result of competition with subsidized food staples from Europe and North America. As proud and aggrieved food producers, they had an automatic gripe with the concept of food security. From their standpoint, food security was all about consumers, not producers. The stock definition of food security refers to the rights of all people to have adequate and proper food. There's no reference to food producers in that definition. It's a shocking omission, perhaps the food equivalent of a Freudian slip that reveals true thoughts – that consumption is such a domineering element of the food system that production is an afterthought, and that there's no need to reference their rights in a definition of food security. If food security spells out the rights of consumer sovereignty, then food sovereignty corrects that imbalance by reasserting the primacy of production.

At a second and deeper level, food sovereignty is about the place of food production in a society and culture. Perhaps there's another blind spot in Northern sensitivity to this. To say that neoliberalism and the WTO are fundamentally about free trade and free markets, as is common in the Global North, avoids the assumption behind the statement — namely, that the world is composed entirely of commodities, and that food is not different from any other commodity. As a matter of fact, this is the official view of the Global North, as evidenced by the Gross National Product (GNP), the standard measuring stick for economic progress. The GNP was developed by an American economist during World War Two as a way to track how much economic energy was going into war production and how much into regular needs apart from war. The same measuring stick was plonked down on the post-War economy, even though GNP takes no measure of the economic value that nature provides – be it clean water or fertile soil or breastmilk. Nor does GNP calculate the economic value of what people are now clamoring to have recognized as 'human capital' or 'cultural capital' or 'social capital' – such factors as quality family time during meals, nutritious foods that increase personal productivity, or increased knowledge and intercultural abilities as a result of being introduced to global food cultures – all of which are overlooked when minds are focused on the commodity value of food. I'm not aware of one government agriculture department that tries to make a tally of food's social, emotional, intellectual, cultural or ecological contribution to the country.

Food sovereignty came on the world scene with its dukes up, ready to take on neoliberals, the WTO, and any NGO members in the Global North who didn't get the point. Inevitably, the tone of discussions was as harsh as the conditions that bred it. But another side of food sovereignty is worth getting to know. It's a side that grew out of deep roots in history, ecology, community and spirituality. It presents a food system that comes from a very different place, a community-based food system.

From the perspective of peasants, fisherfolk, farmers and farmworkers in the Global South, food production is fundamentally about relationships, not commodities that can be bought and sold. Being a peasant, especially for the approximately 500 million peasants of indigenous heritage, is a commitment to ancestral lands, a calling, a connection to a mountain or valley and to the mysterious forces of the universe. These values are interwoven in personal identity, as suggested by such terms of greeting as *campesina* or *paesan*. Over and above economic hardship, the intensity of attachment, identity and belonging felt by people of the land may explain the record high level of suicides in the farming community when farmers confront the prospect of losing their familial land. In India, to give an extreme example, it's estimated that 270,000 farmers have committed suicide since 1995. The suicide rate among farmers tripled after 1995, the year the WTO was launched.[2]

Farming beyond the field

Food production is practiced differently in the North and the South. In the Global North, food production is fundamentally about agriculture. In the Global South, food production is about what's increasingly being called 'agro-ecology'. Protecting a way of farming is part and parcel of protecting a way of life, which is not accounted for either in GNP calculations or in definitions of food security.

The starting-point is that peasants work the land. It's not just that they work it, rather than ride a tractor that works it. They work the land, not a field. There's a world of difference. Agriculture comes from the Latin *ager*, which means field. Wheat, which the Romans branded as the staff of life and of civilization itself, was a field crop. When Europeans colonized much of the world after 1492, they spread a Roman-inspired agriculture based on wheat and fields. That's why Europeans 'conquered the wilderness', as well as the 'savages' who lived in the wilderness, as soon as they began settling and ruling an area. To the European mind, only fields could produce domesticated grains, the staff of life and civilization. Fences were placed at the boundaries of fields, and the inside was intensely managed and ordered. Once food is grown, managed and harvested on a field, it's a relatively small step to make one field the property of one person, and to shunt community property or undomesticated property to the sidelines.

Food producers elsewhere in the world were not particularly drawn to fields or monoculture or to privately owned land. Many fished in lakes and oceans that were owned by no-one. Many gathered fish and sea greens (seaweeds) on common property such as beaches. Others foraged in meadows or forests, looking for food, fuel, fiber for clothes and buildings, and fodder for livestock. Instead of grain-based field crops, some grew root crops, well adapted to tiny clearings in multi-use forests. That's what happened in Brazil, where cassava originated. Other societies had tree crops, sources of the spices that captivated Europeans, or of fruit and nuts. In Peru, where the potato originated, people farmed on terraces they made on the sides of steep mountains. Forests and mountains are not enemies of domesticated food, only resistant to fields, which are really a form of organizing agricultural space as part of the built environment – fields are built for control.

When Europeans, and later Americans, imposed their orderly plantations on colonies in the Global South, they imposed an alien form of field-based food production that had not co-evolved as a partnership connecting people and land. Few have examined exactly how wrenching and brutal was that change in food production methods. Forest-based cultures and religions are different from dryland ones, for example. Community relations are different when resources are managed communally or privately. The human footprint and environmental impacts are different. When farmers clear forests and plough the land, for example, they release carbon. About a third of increased global-warming emissions over the past 150 years come from this one aspect of agricultural clearing, according to the UN Environment Programme report for 2007. Diet is also different in forest- and field-based food production. Field agriculture usually focuses on a few intensively managed crops, while forest foragers graze and nibble on hundreds of foods and medicines.[3] The limited number of outputs of field agriculture – either the wheat crop does well or poorly; either wheat prices are strong or weak – makes it a high-risk/low-resilience option, compared to the diverse and multiple outcomes of a forest.

Food from the forest

With food, as with real estate, the things that count are location, location and location. Food sovereignty comes from a place – from a place in the Global South where non-field food production is commonplace. About 1.6 billion people manage forests for their livelihood, according to the FAO's forestry department. The multiple products available from forests in different seasons make them a haven for people to fall back on whenever times are tough. Likewise, forest work has modest start-up costs – a basket to pick leaves and berries, a drill to tap sap, a knife to cut saplings – nothing expensive, and no need to access credit. A multiple-use forest can be managed as a grocery, pharmacy and hardware store without walls, providing security for the very people most likely to face hunger. Berries, mushrooms, fiber for clothes, wood for building, thatch for roofing, found materials for crafts, fuel, medicine, fodder for livestock: it's the foraging version of multi-tasking. The FAO's Dr Cherukat Chandrasekharan estimated that such renewable non-timber uses of the world's forests contribute $120 billion a year to the economy, on into the indefinite future.[4] That's before these forests contribute such environmental services as storing carbon, preventing soil erosion, and cleaning water that filters down to the water table. The FAO calls this 'non-timber based forestry', but Marcelo Saavedra-Vargas of Bolivia, an Aboriginal Studies expert from the University of Ottawa, says it's a success story of 'non-extractive economics.'

Have you been down to the woods today? Forests are a storehouse of snacks, treats and medicine. Forest honey has more antioxidants than field honey. Tree resin can make chewing gum, such as the chicle (whence Chiclets), which the ancient Mayans took from the sapodilla tree. Chewing gum made from trees is a $10-billion-a-year industry, according to the FAO's *Non-Wood News*. Other treats come from 25,000 tonnes a year of Brazil nuts from the Amazonian rainforest, and 1,300 tonnes of pine nuts from the Kozac area of Turkey, where the forest is also used to graze cattle. Mushrooms and truffles have been rediscovered as gourmet-quality forest crops. For salad greens, try sorrel and spring leaves of willow. Like Canada's wild spring green, fiddleheads, they crop up fast in the spring, before other crops come in. Forests also provide foods with medicinal properties, probably because deep-rooted trees draw scarce minerals to the surface. Ginseng comes from the forest. So does yerba mate, the earthy but mineral-packed tea from the Amazon. So do boars and the original pigs. In Malawi, 37 different species of leafy vegetables, two root vegetables, 21 fruit, 23 mushrooms and 14 varieties of edible caterpillars come from the forest. India has its neem tree, Australia its tea tree, the Philippines its *moringa oleifera*, rich in Vitamin A, C, potassium, calcium, iron and protein. What the forest lacks in volume of crops, it makes up for in diversity of crops – one reason why indigenous and Southern food production link food-medicine-fiber-fuel as one set of linked activities, unlike the system in the Global North, where each is treated as a separate and unrelated function.[5]

A tale of two worlds

Harvard's Edward O Wilson was one of the first celebrity scientists to give this forest economy scientific credibility in the North. The new environmentalists, he wrote in his call to arms, *The Diversity of Life*, won't protect forests by walling them off but by finding 'new ways of drawing income' for people on low incomes who can tap into the wealth of biodiversity. 'The race is on,' he says, 'to draw more income from the wildlands without killing them.' David Waltner-Toews, a leader of Veterinarians without Borders, argues that forests nurture a sense that 'the nature of which we are a part is a kind of flexible, responsive, diverse welfare state'.

Their views match what I saw during a week in 2006 at the Sivananda Yoga Ashram at Neyyar Dam in the Western Ghats, a mountain range in Kerala, India. The state is named after the coconut tree, which people use for 45 different purposes, from food to fuel to medicine to fiber for mats and bags. Typically, a canopy of tall rubber (tapped for use in making surgical gloves) and coconut trees protects smaller fruit and spice trees below, all harvested on an ongoing basis by nearby townsfolk for food, fuel and medicines. The Ashram's Ayurvedic practitioner mixed his preparations from roots and bark of various trees brought to a boil in coconut oil.[6]

In 2007, I met village leaders of two indigenous bands from northern Brazil, the Apakararu and Pataxo, when they visited Toronto. My colleague, Judy New, a North American First Nations nutritionist, immediately reached into a bag for her welcoming gifts, as they spontaneously reached for jewelry made from forest seeds as gifts for her and me. The only white Anglo in the room, I sat on my hands with nothing to contribute, witness to two sharing cultures, separated by thousands of miles and as many years, but based on a common tradition of gift exchange, a commons-based strategy for gaining security through sharing rather than private appropriation.

The 'wild west' style takeover of Brazil's indigenous lands forced members of the two bands to relocate to an isolated and protected area in the north, where they are organizing their village around concentric circles of different foods. Manioc (cassava) will be grown close to their homes; further away will be bushes laden with berries and materials for crafts; yet further out will be trees for nuts, firewood and lumber: their leader, Toe, shows me all this on a map. Manioc was first grown by Brazil's indigenous forest peoples, and features leaves and roots rich in protein, phosphorus, calcium and Vitamin C. The attention to food planning is obvious as they prepare their move to the new village. Food is central to maintaining indigenous identity, says Geralda Soares, their researcher and translator. They eat common foods – manioc, melons, sweet potatoes, corn and fish. They work communally to prepare the fields, harvest the crops and celebrate their successes. 'Food is life. It is not just land, but culture, history and geography,' she says.

Forest gardens are an effort to domesticate and mimic the productivity and diversity of nature's forests in small yards. In 2012, I toured one in Yorito, a small village near the rugged mountains of Honduras. Innovative farmer-researcher teams (known as CIALs) encourage people to grow forest gardens as a way to expand their diets beyond corn and beans, and as a way for people in the community to take their own power. We ate our meals in the dining room of Nelba Velasquez, a micro-entrepreneur who also runs a small water-purification plant next door which is staffed by young single moms, a landscaping shop and a quarter-acre forest garden behind her home that she's tended for 26 years. When I walk into her backyard, I feel the cool of being in the woods, and feel like I'm looking at the answer to climate instability, hunger and malnutrition close to home. Beside a hammock, a sink, a baking oven, a clothes line and a showcase for landscaping plants is an odorless compost heap based on a Japanese recipe that CIAL promotes called Bokachi, which is made with banana leaves, limestone, molasses, yeast, manure, carbon and ashes from burned wood – all common household waste and designed to boost soil productivity. Here's what's in Velasquez's forest: four avocado trees, 11 guava trees, a papaya tree, a mandarin orange tree, a lemon tree, a nance tree (with bright yellow berries), a plum tree, 60 coffee plants, a tamarind tree, an allspice tree, 10 banana trees, passion fruit, sweet grass, raised beds with beans, squash, zucchini, chayote (a kind of gourd) and celery. 'I always want to diversify everything,' says Velasquez, who's also on the local health board and executive of her local CIAL, which promotes diversity as a tool for empowerment. 'My hands are in everything.'

It's no surprise that forest foragers of the Global South see themselves and food sovereignty as part of a fight for life. Edward O Wilson estimates that the world's forests have been shrinking at a rate of two per cent a year since 1950. The pace is picking up. In Africa, South America and Indonesia, forest losses have been significant, threatening the forest food economy. Africa's forest cover declined from 699 to 635 million hectares between 1990 and 2005, while in South America coverage went from 891 to 832 million hectares. Since 2005, many more millions of hectares of forest have been slashed to make way for simplified plantations of palm trees to produce biofuels for cars that will likely be marketed as 'green'.[7]

Meadows, beaches – and insects

Meadows and wild grasslands harbor as many overlooked food, medicinal, fuel, fiber and fodder sources as forests. Some foods are wild plants and herbs that farmers (who call them weeds) want out of their fields. Many weeds are a nutritionist's field of dreams. Dandelions are a powerhouse of vitamins A and C, as well as minerals such as calcium, potassium, silicon and magnesium. Purslane, Gandhi's favorite vegetable, is rich in iron, lack of which causes one of the most common and debilitating mineral deficiencies in the world. Stinging nettles are rich in B vitamins. Pigweed is a variant of protein-rich amaranth. Wild groundnut tubers are high in protein and immune-building isoflavones – 'Mother Nature's grocery store,' one weed enthusiast claims.[8]

Like the forest, the open meadow is a buddy to people facing hard times. Leaves and stems of wild plants are tastiest in early spring salads, before domesticated greens have roused from their sleep. Dried seeds, nice in baked goods, are there in the late fall, after harvest is done. Wild plants are low-maintenance. Meadows are a no-till, no GE, no pesticide and fertilizer-free zone, which may account for their lack of promoters among the farm-input industries. The commons are a workshop for common people. Admission is free. But they do require labor and knowledge, resources that are plentiful. Government anti-poverty programs could well duplicate such empowering conditions.

Ocean beaches offer another food and pharmaceutical commons, ideal for finding nutrient-rich greens, reds and browns, sometimes called seaweeds. I had a cook's tour of an ocean beach with marine biologist Irene Novaczek when I was volunteering on an organic farm in Prince Edward Island, on Canada's east coast, in 2007.

As well as leading the Island Institute, which partners with indigenous peoples in Chile to help them recover their healthy seaplant dietary traditions, Novaczek runs her own company, Oceanna Seaplants, which makes medicinal teas and creams from plants washed up on the beach. She introduced me to the intricacies of what experts call 'phycophagy' or 'marine algae', as she talked up her favorite sea vegetables – gracilaria, sugar kelp and wrack, all loaded with manganese, zinc and iodine, and all easy to slip into soups, salads or puddings.

A tale of two worlds

The Cambridge World History of Food identifies sea plants as rich sources of protein, iodine and phenols, as well as essential fatty acids. More recently, a study in the *Journal of Nutrition* identified several varieties of seaweed as excellent sources of iron that the body can use easily. Seaplants were a central part of the human diet prior to the rise of agriculture, and continue to define many cuisines, most famously Japanese and Korean cuisines, which feature seaplants in salads, broths and wrapped around sushi.[9]

As with all foods from the commons, seaplants are free to those who invest time and effort, but depend on traditional knowledge that is usually developed and shared among women, and passed on as mother and child work the beaches together. Such traditional knowledge is vulnerable to extinction, however, Novaczek says, and is lost when it's not used. 'We need to work with the natural resources at hand and live within our means,' she says.

Entomophagy is another way to work the commons for food, still popular in most of the world. Ants, termites, locusts, grasshoppers, crickets, beetles, caterpillars and moths are among some 2,000 species of insects enjoyed as snacks and delicacies in various countries. Ohio State University extension programs identify insects as micro-livestock. According to *The Cambridge World History of Food*, sago grubs wrapped in banana leaves and roasted over an open fire get rave reviews in Papua New Guinea, while large queen leafcutter ants are a delicacy in Colombia, and bee brood and honeycomb wrapped in banana leaves are hot in Thailand. Oaxaca, one of the culinary capitals of Mexico, makes a specialty of grasshoppers, sold at several stands of the farmers' market all dressed up with salt and powdered chili. I munched a sandwich filled with about 25 of them in a restaurant overlooking the city square, while Oaxaca's leading public intellectual, Gustavo Esteva, regaled me with stories of indigenous culture. Nutritionists will be bug-eyed to know that caterpillars match beef, pork, and chicken in protein, show stronger on iron, zinc, niacin, thiamine and riboflavin, and win hands-down in ratings for low cholesterol and high essential fats.

In a 2004 report for the FAO, Paul Vantomme identifies insects as a 'forgotten food crop' for the poor and disadvantaged. In many African villages, he says, trees are planted strategically to attract insects for a two-month period when they're rearing their young, which makes for easy pickings – the insect equivalent of low-hanging fruit. As with sea plants, field greens and forest snacks, women and children do the work without any owners or managers over them. The marginalizing of these food sources by field or plantation agriculture is a study in the ways Northern land-use practices imposed huge opportunity costs by overlooking food sources outside their range of vision. We are what we don't eat.[10]

Essential to survival

According to Edward O Wilson, people have eaten some 7,000 species of plants. That is a fraction of nature's smorgasbord, which offers 30,000 edible species. 'Modern agriculture is only a sliver of what it could be,' Wilson writes in *The Diversity of Life*. 'Waiting in the wings are tens of thousands of unused plant species, many demonstrably superior to those in favor,' such as the delicious lulo fruit of Colombia and Ecuador, or the winged bean of New Guinea, a 'one species supermarket'. Given Wilson's view on the abundance of food choices provided by nature, it is no surprise that he is a critic of the conventional view that hunger comes from lack of money. People do not die for lack of income, he argues, but lack of access to the wealth of the commons. There's the rub: many of the 7,000 species that humans have nibbled on, and most of the 23,000 species they overlook, live in that no-one's land known as the commons, and therefore lack any commercial value for corporations.[11]

A tale of two worlds

Many people in the South look upon the forest, meadow or seashore commons as something akin to a part-time job: a place to work during free time on off-season or slow days. Among people who live close to the edge, the food income from such part-time work makes all the difference for survival. For that reason, food from the commons is often called 'survival food'. When people gather foods from the commons, they also gain access to a wide range of foods and nutrients they don't get from their day job, which usually centers on a small number of staple crops. That makes commons food crucial to health, not just survival. Because knowledge to work the commons descends from a female folk culture, the foods are also crucial for maintaining popular traditions and women's esteem.

Such physical and cultural survival issues are most poignant in Africa, the continent most colonized by plants and livestock from other continents. Experts fear Africa faces a 'genetic meltdown', and risks losing 2,000 livestock breeds and plants uniquely adapted to the climatic challenges it faces in the coming era of global warming. Since indigenous foods have no appeal to markets in the Global North, commercial growers don't bother saving them. The commons stand between these breeds and extinction. For example, Kenyan ethno-botanist Patrick Maundu campaigns to save the food birthright of 'African spinach' – hundreds of varieties of green leaves, many snipped from the commons in the 'cut and come again' tradition that allows repeated harvests from the same plants. Jeopardizing the future of this spinach undermines both nutrition and the crucial role of women gatherers, he says.[12]

In India and Bangladesh, the health benefits of access to the commons led to a comprehensive rethink of food policy. Supporters of the New Agricultural Movement based in the floodplains of Bangladesh, and of the Deccan Development Society based in the dry plateau of southern India, say the issue is 'the politics of weeds'.

In 2007, Farhad Mazhar and colleagues reported on approximately 100 'uncultivated foods' that nourish people and livestock. Poor women take leaves from pumpkins and gourds in farmed fields, and leaves from other plants that are found beside laneways or around fences – wherever an orphaned patch of land is not owned by an individual, and has come to be accepted as public space. About 65 per cent of the food, fuel and fodder of poor villagers, and about 34 per cent of the needs of more affluent villagers, come from such spaces. Anti-poverty programs should be based on these successes, the Mazhar team says. 'In our view, the failure of poverty-alleviation schemes is due to an overemphasis on income and employment initiatives and a profound disregard for expenditure-saving activities,' they argue. Since public access to the means of livelihood is vital for everyone in a village, food sovereignty, or community control over local resources, becomes the question of the hour. Mazhar's team believes that three contributors to community control of food – biodiversity, local control and women-centered knowledge – are under threat by the WTO. Community rights to make food production 'a life-affirming practice and deeply human undertaking' need to be asserted, they write. Likewise, food needs to be appreciated as more than a utility that staves off hunger. Food is 'a joy of life, produced and eaten not only to satisfy hunger, but also to savor and share with others in the community', they write.[13]

This is where we get to the heart of the matter with the problem food sovereignty lays at the doorstep of the WTO and neoliberalism. Of course, food sovereigntists have a problem with allowing subsidies to European and American exporters but disallowing protective measures against subsidized exports. But their biggest issue is with the WTO and neoliberal principle that all things food are commodities, and none deserve special protection just because they are central to culture, community or spirituality. Food sovereignty resonates with the lived experience of gathering food, and with the customary rights of hundreds of millions of ordinary people. Social history shows that the most passionate rebellions of the most humble peoples have almost always broken out when customary rights seem in jeopardy. That is the proverbial line in the sand. During the 1990s and early 2000s, when peasants in Asia and Africa worried that their well-being and community values were threatened by changes, they coined a phrase to express an assumed right – 'food sovereignty', which stood on guard for their commons, source of both collective and individual food security.

Agro-ecology

When it comes to actual food production, rather than foraging and gathering, I ask Claudia Ho Lem for an introduction to the Philippines and China, where she worked in 2003 for a Canadian NGO called Resource Efficient Agricultural Production. 'It's no accident that agro-ecology comes out of the Global South,' says Ho Lem, an effervescent Canadian of mixed Polish, Chinese and First Nations descent. In the South, people need to recover their pre-European heritage of crops and land-use patterns that was more in tune with the seasons. In northern countries like Canada, we always think the people in the tropical South have an easy time of it, with no freezing winters to put up with. In fact, one season of torrential monsoon rainfall is followed by a dry season, each more challenging to respond to than Canadian summers and winters. Agro-ecology is the form of food production best suited to their challenges.

Climate matters. Food production happens on a planet with variations in every region. When monsoon rains strike the ground directly, the force is so powerful that it flushes out soil and nutrients, overloading water bodies with nutrients and killing the fish. Tropical forests adapted to this challenge with an overstory of tall trees with broad leaves to break the rainfall, below which were a series of shorter trees, bushes and ground plants that let the water trickle down gently, thereby preventing erosion of nutrients needed by plants and harmful to fish. Enter the Europeans, replacing diverse forests with monoculture field crops of sugar cane, bananas and pineapple. These plants took advantage of tropical heat, but didn't protect the soil or waterways from erosion.

To heal the colonial legacy, the Global South needs fundamental changes in land-use, crop choices and land-water relationships, Hem Lo tells me. That's where agro-ecology comes in. It designs for multiple outcomes of food, fuel and fiber, and so can offer a wider palette of options than heat-loving foods for export markets. With local self-reliance and ecosystem management as their goal instead of exports, a community-minded design of diverse plants can restore balance and sustainability to a tropical food system.

Ho Lem's backgrounder on climate and food strategy prepared me for the story I saw unfold before my eyes when I was in Goa, India, in December 2006. The day we arrived in this normally quiet, tourist-oriented state, there was a mass demonstration against Babush (a first name with letters that stand for bold, achieving, brilliant, understanding, simple and humble, his admirers said in a newspaper ad) Monserrate, the senior politician making real-estate deals with resorts in the area – often by selling lands long occupied by tenant farmers, who were promptly sent packing. Daily protests continued for a week, the sense of betrayal growing in the community with each passing day. 'If these atrocities continue, then the whole village will burn down the project,' one protester said. In short order, the brilliant but humble Monserrate resigned from office.

Looking for a way to explain the popular militancy I saw, I picked up a book called *The Goan Village Communes* by a local academic, Olivinho Gomes. It turns out that locals have been organized in village communes for over 2,000 years. Villagers worked as a team to build structures to store monsoon rainfall for later use in irrigation. According to Gomes, this village commune tradition was the 'bedrock of the Goan identity'. Treating land as a private commodity rather than community utility didn't fit with the food system needed in a Southern climate. That's why villagers always resisted 'pernicious politicians who have transformed themselves into downright mercenary interests' and defended land-use rules that benefited everyone. That tradition was revived in 2006.[14]

I suspect that a similar process was at work at exactly the same time in West Bengal, where the government was confiscating farmland to give away for a Tata Motors car factory. Dissident politician Mamata Banerjee launched a 25-day hunger strike to protest this land grab and gained national publicity.[15]

Whether it's for tourist resorts or factories, almost any business can pay more money for land than farmers can. Without powerful values that place farmland on a community pedestal, farmland near towns and cities can always be sold to a higher bidder. This is why community food security and food sovereignty move to the forefront when land grabs happen. If food and farming are seen as business decisions, not community survival decisions, no land is safe from a higher bidder. The real value of foodlands is not measured by the sale price of a food commodity, but the use value of fresh, local and accessible food. Efforts to seize land for tourist resorts, dams, mines and factories always tempt investors in the Global South because the cost of land is pegged to peasant uses, which yield no meaningful profits. To protect these foodlands and to protect land values that make food affordable, communities need to assert community control over land use – which just happens to be a priority for La Via Campesina and the food sovereignty movement.

Land or death

I remember Hugo Blanco from the 1960s, when his fierce portrait under the slogan 'Land or Death' gained him an international reputation as a heroic fighter for Peruvian peasants struggling for land. In 1963, Blanco was sentenced to death for organizing a peasant land seizure, but the international campaign won his freedom. When I heard he'd come to Toronto in 2007, I had to meet this fiery revolutionist. He looked out at the audience with a toothy grin beaming from beneath a floppy sheepskin hat, the kind worn by indigenous Quechua people in Peru's frigid mountains. At 72, he was under strict orders from his doctor to keep that hat on, for fear that his skull has already endured so many police beatings that it can't take one more bump now.

Even though he looks like a huggable grandpa, Blanco's opening line took me by surprise. Indigenous politics in South America are feisty today, 500 long years after Europeans invaded, he says, because mining, oil and gas corporations have finally crossed the line. 'They are poisoning *Pachamama*, Mother Earth,' he says, and their greed threatens '*ayllu*', the indigenous sense of community that includes every being in the village, including hills, rivers, animals, plants and vegetables, each endowed with one or more spirits. The combined destruction of Nature and community strikes 'aggressively against the two chords of our culture,' Blanco said, which the people must defend or lose forever.

'I struggle to break free from European ideas stuck in my head,' Blanco says, 'and to recover my indigenous identity.' One of Blanco's daughters, herself raised in Sweden during one of his many exiles, led Swedish tourists through a Peruvian village and was told that it looked like Swedish socialism. You have that backwards, she told them; Swedish socialism looks like this. Blanco has also changed his ideas about power. 'Among revolutionaries, we were negatively affected by obsession with power,' he says, but now, in keeping with indigenous traditions, 'we are not about taking power, but building power from below.' He likes to organize 'peasant circles', which displace judges and corrupt government officials with self-managing groups.

After the talk, I luck into a two-hour dinner with Blanco, Phil Cournoyer, the translator of his memoirs, and assorted friends at a nearby internet café serving Somali food. When Blanco chanted Land or Death, he already had 'an incipient understanding' that he was saying something different from the popular Cuban cry, Fatherland or Death, Cournoyer says. As an indigenous person, Blanco felt that land was linked to identity, meaning and life – not just a nation-state in struggle against an empire. 'It is not the earth that belongs to the people, but the people who belong to the earth,' Blanco adds. From the global leader of militant land reform during the 1960s comes a 21st-century vision of land, raised in the soil where food sovereignty was also reared.

In his seventies, Blanco remains active as editor of *La Lucha Indigena* ('The Indigenous Struggle'). He published the entire text of the Cochabamba Declaration, adopted by an indigenous conference in Bolivia on 12 October 2007, which celebrated the UN declaration of rights for the world's 370 million indigenous peoples, most of whom live in the Global South. The declaration hails a new 'millennium of life, of balance, and wholeness, without having to abuse energies that destroy Mother Earth', and calls on governments to 'implement national policies for food sovereignty as the main basis of national sovereignty in which the community guarantees both respect for its own culture and its places and ways of carrying our production, distribution and consumption in harmony with the nature of healthy, uncontaminated food available to all, eliminating hunger because alimentation is a life right'.[16]

Land grabs

Until the 1990s, one of the most wrenching decades of modern history, traditional village patterns of the Global South survived, protected to some extent by benign neglect on the part of outside forces. The long arm of the World Trade Organization ended isolation from the outside world, and forced peasants to define and defend their way of life, their community foodways, and their choice of a vision of the future.

The principles behind food sovereignty may have gelled during the 1990s in response to this neoliberal agenda identified with the WTO, but they have remained somewhat timeless, not tied to any one grudge or one fixed idea and vision. The activities and campaigns inspired by food sovereignty continue to respond to new issues of the day. Beginning around 2008, a new issue of 'land grabs' became the galvanizing issue of peasant and small farmer rights.

According to the globally respected charity Oxfam, since 2001, foreign speculators have bought up and taken over some 227 million hectares of land, roughly equal to the size of Western Europe, in Africa, South America and Asia. The purchases are commonly referred to as land grabs because the deals were cut between investors and politicians who sold lands that were not theirs to sell. A defining feature of a land grab, as distinct from a typical real-estate transaction, is that land is taken without the knowledge, participation or agreement of longstanding residents, who are forced to leave the land, often violently, when the new owners give the order.[17] Those who see the historical parallel with how North and South America were expropriated by European empires refer to this phase of massive land grab as 'the new imperialism'.

There are several explanations for the rise of land grabs, especially since 2008. The sudden leap in the world price for food staples in 2007 and 2008, followed by years of slower price increases, convinced several countries – including China, South Korea, and Saudi Arabia – that their future food security depended on buying land that could be devoted exclusively to feeding them. The continuing rise in prices also convinced speculators that there could be a handsome return on investment in land, especially land with easy access to irrigation, which describes most of the land that has been grabbed. Even speculators who didn't predict continuing high prices for food knew that land was at least a safe place to park money when internet stocks, housing bubbles and banks seemed less than stable. Another group of investors hopes to cash in on biofuels made from plantations of palm trees and similar oil-rich plants. Oddly enough, much-needed infrastructure projects, requiring hundreds of billions of dollars in investment, languish, while the big money is going to land deals that are 'taking the only resource of the poorest people in the world,' says investigative reporter Joan Baxter. She notes that when people from entire African villages are evicted, they have no other village in the country to go to because most small villages have a kin structure that prevents large-scale migration, so the evicted often end up in African slums or as migrant laborers in Europe.

Major groups campaigning on this issue, including Oxfam and people around the magazine *Grain*, argue that the rights of local communities – where smallholder farmers descend from families that worked the land back in the mists of time, before there was formal legal title – be given priority in any disputes. This notion of community control rooted in food production continues to have 'legs' in the policy realm. It's worth recognizing that this understanding of food issues and food system planning was first brought to public attention by promoters of food sovereignty, after a period of neglect in the thinking around food security.

Pat Mooney of ETC Group is one of the people who picked up my spirits and helped me through my first international conference, back in 2002. After a long day of meetings at the FAO offices in Rome, he took me to a nice little place near the Spanish Steps, walking there as if he knew it by heart. After dinner he ordered ice cream, and I looked over to see him hold the bowl exactly the way my mother, who was blind, held her bowl. Mooney has worked the back rooms of international conferences since the 1980s, using his photographic memory to share important information, and then cajoling people to try partnering with someone who can help move the agenda forward. He may be blind, but he was one of the first to see food systems and so can see further than most. He is also one of the first to push work on plant breeding that can respond to the enormous challenges of what's called global warming, but could equally be called global droughting, global hurricaning, or global pest infestations – whatever combination prevails will require plant breeders to adapt. And that's where Mooney sees food sovereignty playing its role, protecting those people who are better at seed innovation than any other – peasants.

Mooney rattled off the numbers to me from memory. At present, the work being done on genetic and crop biodiversity is frightfully narrow. First, 76 per cent of research in the area is controlled by six companies – Mooney calls it The Joy of Six: Monsanto, Dupont, Syngenta, Bayer, BASF and Dow – the same level of corporate concentration that ran the oil industry for most of its history. These six companies, without any consultation with the public or government or any accountability to the public interest, concentrate their resources narrowly. Their work on fish is limited to four species. Their work on animals is focused on four breeds, all heavy consumers of resources. Half their plant research is focused on corn. Their research costs are high – averaging $136 million to complete the work on one seed variety. Even champions of biotechnology such as the Gates Foundation find the cost of such innovation is far too rich, and don't sink much money in it. 'We can't get where we need to go from here,' says Mooney.

On the other hand, peasants, contrary to their reputation as belonging in and looking to the past, have a track record for innovation. Perhaps the greatest period of genetic diversification in agriculture during the short span of human history is known as the 'Columbian exchange', when domesticated plants from the Americas – corn (maize), potatoes, cassava, tomatoes, cocoa to name the best-known – spread around the world within a hundred years, thanks to peasant innovators. The same was true for about 50 plants from Africa – coffee, cowpeas, black-eyed peas, okra and sorghum, as well as rice varieties hidden in the hair of women as they crossed the ocean on slave ships, when Africans were enslaved to labor on plantations in the Americas.

Peasants and small farmers can perform the same miracles again, says Mooney. They work with 7,000 plant species, 84,000 breeds of land animals and 22,000 maritime species. They raise the food eaten by two-thirds of the world's population, using only 25 per cent of the planet's agricultural lands.

'History shows they can do it amazingly rapidly,' he says. 'If they can keep diversity, we will survive global climate change. If not, we won't. It's as simple as that.' Not a bad reason to think that food sovereignty is an idea for the future.

1 The earliest I've seen it issued is in G. Esteva, 'Four Needs and Capacities: Four Centuries of Conflict,' in J Austin, G Esteva, eds, *Food Policy in Mexico*, Cornell, 1982. **2** W Stephenson, 'Indian farmers and suicide' *BBC News*, 22 Jan 2013; P Behere, M Bhise, 'Farmers' suicide: Across culture,' *Indian Journal of Psychiatry*, 2009 Oct-Dec, 51 (4). **3** 'Deforestation, Climate Change Magnify East African Drought,' at nin.tl/16Ef9Mu ; United Nations Environment Programme, GEO4, Progress Press, 2007, p 100. **4** FAO, *non-wood news*, Jul 2007. **5** See generally, the FAO publication, *non-wood news*, and the Community Forestry Resource Centre, both accessible online. **6** Brian Griffith, *The Gardens of Their Dreams,* Fernwood, 2001; D Waltner-Toews, *The Chickens Fight Back*, Greystone, 2007, p 60. **7** 'Forest Cover Indicator 1990-2005,' at Earth Policy Institute, www.earthpolicy.org **8** W Roberts,

Get A Life! (Toronto, 1995); T Dean, 'Stalking the Wild Groundnut,' *Orion Magazine*, November-December, 2007; see also Steve Brill website www.wildmanstevebrill.com **9** Food Navigator.com 23 Nov 2007, citing research in *Journal of Nutrition*, Dec 2007; for sources and intricacies of seaplants, see W Roberts, 'Fishsticks these ain't,' *This Magazine*, Nov-Dec 2007. **10** For sources and more examples, see W Roberts, 'Eating Insects: Waiter, there's no fly in my soup,' *Alternatives Journal*, Jan 2008. **11** EO Wilson, *The Diversity of Life* (Harvard University Press, 1992), pp 287-9. **12** BBC posting, on listserv, soilandhealth 4 Sep 2007; Environmental News Service, 3 Sep 2007; *Common Dreams*, 5 Sep 2007; FAO, 'The State of the World's Animal Genetic Resources,' posted on FoodNews 12 Sep 2007; nin.tl/14xedFF ; and nin.tl/16EfOOb **13** F Mazhar, *Food Sovereignty and Uncultivated Biodiversity in South Asia*, Academic Foundation, 2007, available at www.irdc.ca/openbooks **14** *Indian Express*, 19 Dec 2006; *Panjim Herald*, 20 Dec 2006; *Gomantak Times*, 23 Dec 2006; OJ Gomes, *The Goan Village Communes*, Vasantrao Dempo Education and Research Foundation, 2005. **15** *Navind Times*, 25 Dec 2006; Mumbai *Hindustan Times*, 27 Dec 2006; India News Online, 1 Jan 2007. **16** 'Indigenous Peoples of South America Adoption of UN Declaration on the Rights of Indigenous Peoples,' translated by P Cournoyer, posted by *Foodnews* 6 Oct 2007. **17** Oxfam International, *Land and Power*, briefing paper, 22 Sep 2011.

5 Bread and roses: overcoming hunger

About one person in seven around the world suffers regularly from hunger, some in North America and Europe, but mostly in Asia, Africa and South America. This chapter reviews successful efforts in two countries and one small town to overcome hunger. A diet rich in empowerment and participation seems to be the precondition for success.

Something about world hunger doesn't add up. Anyone who does the math agrees there's no rational explanation why hunger should blight the life of one person in seven on this planet. There's more than enough food for everyone, study after study shows. And apart from the ethics of allowing so many to go hungry, the sheer economic burden of tolerating hunger cries out for remedial action. The World Bank estimates that just one disorder, anemia caused by shortage of iron, costs businesses $50 billion a year in lost productivity. Governments in the developing world could stop that problem dead in its tracks by dedicating 0.4 per cent of their GNP to providing 500 calories a day worth of food to people going without. The World Food Programme calls proper nutrition for all a 'best buy in today's tough economy', and describes hunger as 'the world's greatest solvable problem'.[1] In a 2005 report, the FAO promoted anti-hunger investments as the key to achieving all the United Nations Millennium Development Goals (MDGs). Overcoming hunger, the FAO report argued, advances all eight goals – eradicate extreme poverty, promote universal primary education, empower women, reduce child mortality, improve maternal health, combat infectious disease, ensure environmental sustainability, and encourage global development partnerships.[2]

The mismatch between what could be done to eliminate hunger and what is actually done has led many, such as former FAO leader Jacques Diouf, to claim the missing link needed to end hunger was not shortage of food but lack of 'political will.'[3] That's become a standard view among those who have counted the real abundance of food and the real costs of hunger. It is, however, rather naïve. Although the tolerance for persistent hunger violates both ethics and economics, there's more to overcoming bad ethics or bad economics than political will.

First, it takes more than willful determination, or even money, to end hunger. It takes skill in designing good programs. Some of these skills will be demonstrated in this chapter based on three reasonably successful efforts to deal with hunger from different starting-points.

Second, popular will needs to be strong enough to overcome the will of powerful groups that benefit from dealings that cause hunger. A food system based on selling and trading commodities, rather than providing health, community or environmental service, lurks behind hunger. Governments in the Global North plough hundreds of billions of dollars of public money into subsidies for food exports to the Global South, as well as maintaining regulations keeping Southern food exports out of the North. Calculations by the Organization for Economic Co-operation and Development indicate that rich countries spend roughly seven times more money on tilting the playing field to the disadvantage of the Global South than they do on aid.[4] That's why the first skill-set needed by governments and organizations genuinely working to reduce hunger is the know-how to empower people who are hungry.

The policy rationale for that skill-set comes from Amartya Sen, who won the Nobel Prize in economics for his studies of famines. Famines are not caused by lack of food, Sen argues, but by lack of rights. When people blame famines on natural disasters, they miss the real problem – a social disaster caused by a shortage of rights. 'Hunger is a many-headed monster,' his argument goes. People suffering from hunger are also often suffering from racism, sexism, deep poverty, illiteracy, lack of healthcare, water, jobs and good land, as well as lack of money to buy food. Confront these fellow travelers of hunger, and famines become so easy to manage 'that it is amazing that they are allowed to occur at all.' Sometimes preventing hunger can be as easy as sponsoring public-works programs that pay members of at-risk groups so they can buy the food they need from nearby farmers. Dealing with the social vulnerability that accompanies such disadvantage is a hallmark of dynamic programs confronting both famine and hunger.[5]

Before we get to the case studies, I should define hunger. Many people say they're hungry if they skipped breakfast and are looking forward to lunch. For the one person in seven across the world classified as hungry, that would be utopia. Hunger is traditionally defined as lacking the calories and protein to maintain body functioning during an active day. Hunger is also closely connected to malnutrition, a lack of micronutrients and trace minerals that protect health over the long term. The successes I review here are based on respecting people's need for overall nutrition.

Cuban city farms

I figured I was easy enough to spot – a balding Gringo standing on the steps of Havana's Capitol Building, holding onto 30 meters of garden hose. The hose was something that my host Roberto Pérez Rivero had asked me to bring along as a donation to a children's garden – a good introduction to the everyday things missing in Cuba and to the entrepreneurial deal-making Cubans bring to conventional socialism as they seek ways to feed themselves from city gardens. But I had no idea how to spot Pérez Rivero, the informal ambassador for urban agriculture in Cuba and a leader of the country's

Antonio Núñez Jiménez Foundation for Nature and Humanity. No problem. Wearing shorts, a T-shirt and fresh sunburn, he waved at me right away. I decided to take a day off and go to the beach, he said, and off we went to a restaurant specializing in Cuban-style Chinese food.

Pérez Rivero's group was launched in 1994, hard times still referred to as the 'special period' – when Cuba's bedrock of economic support, the Soviet Union, collapsed. His organization was one among what Pérez Rivero calls an 'NGO boom', when activists formed some 3,000 organizations to raise money from international donors to fund their pioneering work. Cubans went hungry when delivery of Russian oil and grains and Russian purchases of Cuban sugar and oranges ground to a halt. An average person who ate 2,900 calories a day during the 1980s suddenly had to survive on 1,863 calories in 1994, less than bodies need for a healthy and active life. On a spectrum from available to accessible, Cuba faced a classic availability crisis. There

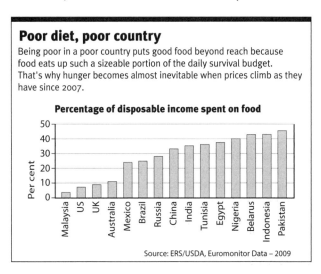

Poor diet, poor country

Being poor in a poor country puts good food beyond reach because food eats up such a sizeable portion of the daily survival budget. That's why hunger becomes almost inevitable when prices climb as they have since 2007.

Percentage of disposable income spent on food

Source: ERS/USDA, Euromonitor Data – 2009

wasn't enough being produced to go around, no matter how it was distributed.

The government gave leeway to people like Pérez Rivero to explore frontier ideas to address the crisis. Instead of insisting on state-owned farms, the government let the unemployed become self-employed garden entrepreneurs, selling what they grew on public lands at farmers' markets. This change could not have been easy. Cuba's old-line Communism had been spellbound by 1950s modernist ideals of high-tech, high-input farming in state-run and worker collectives. Giving the green light to independent NGOs and small entrepreneurs was a sea change in the government's approach to food and agriculture.

Pérez Rivero was in his element. In his twenties, he got to sow his wild oats during a Renaissance of bold experimentation. I grew up thinking there were three choices, he told me – a society controlled by the market, by the state, or by community groups. To test the waters, he founded a magazine called *It's Possible*, which sums up his approach.

Holding to egalitarian principles, the government shared the burdens of hard times fairly evenly, rationing food and other necessities, and cutting back on luxuries. Meals were no frills – beans, peas, rice, a little meat, no fruits or vegetables, and no treats except loads of sugar, which was plentiful. Some cuts to luxuries really hurt – especially the limit of three bouquets of flowers per funeral. Community gardeners saw the business opportunity, and started growing flowers. They were in a grand tradition, launched in 1912 by two teenage girls on strike against a New Jersey textile factory. On the picket line, the girls carried a placard with their own hand-written message that became a global symbol of how horizons of hope grow when people in poverty move forward in a common cause: 'We want bread and we want roses.'

Cuba had to overcome more than the loss of Soviet

cash subsidies. Cuba also lost its lifeline to low-cost fossil fuels that powered the tractors on rural state farms and the trucks that brought food to the city, where the great majority of Cubans lived. Sheer necessity was in charge now, and the entire architecture of food production and distribution had to follow dictates of change.

Cuba's campaign to prevent hunger was based on promotion of *organopónicos*, urban organic gardens growing more fruits and vegetables. Cuba has long been a highly urban country. It was more fuel-efficient to move food production into the city than to transport food from country to city, and keep it chilled during transit. Cuba's agricultural practices were almost as mechanized and fertilizer- and pesticide-dependent – another way of saying oil-dependent – as those of the US, and had to go cold turkey without such inputs. The city is wealthier in waste products that can become farm inputs – most obviously compost from food scraps, which can replace fertilizers, and at the same time save the fuel to run garbage trucks that once picked up food scraps and hauled them far away – a two-for-one efficiency. Cities are also ideal for growing foods that should be the mainstay of the diet of mostly sedentary city people – vegetables and fruit. Rural areas are suited to grow grains, carbs and meat that take a lot of space, and the intense labor on many farms requires a diet that supplies lots of energy. But compact cities where people can't afford refrigerators are a good match with compact fruit and vegetable gardens that can offer perishable foods in small quantities that can be bought fresh daily.

Pérez Rivero describes the traditional Cuban diet as 'redundant in carbohydrates' – as in white rice, sugar and sugared drinks. Before the 'special period', obesity rates in Cuba ran at 30 per cent, then fell to 16 per cent as a result of food deprivation. City farming became an opportunity to wean Cubans off empty, calorie-dense carbs, and onto nutrient-dense, calorie-light fruits and vegetables. Because of low world prices for sugar, the government actually shut down sugar mills and some 400,000 hectares of sugar plantations, making the land available for food production. But persuading people to switch to greens took a lot of sweet talking. Pérez Rivero remembers that many early gardeners dismissed greens as weeds and rabbit food. His organization put on both nutrition and cooking classes.

The output of vegetables from some 383,000 city farms tripled during the 1990s, part of a fast-paced increase in food production (up 4.2 per cent a year) throughout society. City farms moved food closer to the people by supplying over 70 per cent of vegetables eaten in the city. The overriding purpose of Cuba's agricultural revolution was to prevent hunger in the face of energy shortage, and organic was valued as a low-energy production method more than as a counter-cultural statement about food purity. City location, organic (low-energy) methods, nutritious foods and hunger prevention: all of these co-evolved as an integrated whole.

Some city plots were designed for people who had lost their jobs and were looking into gardening as a career. Other plots, often on the grounds of hospitals, schools and workplaces, grew food for staff and clients. Still others provisioned neighborhoods, while others produced for farmers' markets. All told, gardens take up about 12 per cent of Havana's space.

Pérez Rivero provides training for people working small lots to supply an immediate neighborhood – part of a plan to have one plot for every 15 housing units. He takes me to a small home in a low-income area. A yard behind the house features several piles of truck tires that have been filled with composted soil and converted into planters. An old bathtub is another container. The more containers there are, the merrier the intensive gardening; plants can grow higher, and they can droop, allowing containers to double the production in small places. Overhead are two roof gardens loaded with tires and pots. I spot papaya, guava, onions, spinach, grapes (one roof is given over to them alone), oregano, pomegranate, sweet pepper, aloe, tomatoes and basil. He expects the three six- by six-meter gardens here can contribute significantly to five families.

Cuba's first success was to overcome the severe shortages of the special period and to do so without relying on food imports that the economy couldn't afford. Cuba has become more than 80-per-cent self-sufficient.[6] In the next phase, the challenge will be to move beyond accepting the necessities imposed by lack of fuel and money to embracing the opportunities to promote nutrition, food production methods adapted to Cuba's terroir, dishes for a unique Cuban cuisine, and crops adapted to the special risks the country faces in terms of hurricanes and other destructive results of global warming.

Pérez Rivero is happy that the special period is not special any more. 'We need to get rid of the label that this is because of an emergency,' he says. Collecting food scraps and containers for urban gardens isn't just for hard times. 'If we manage garbage properly, we get rid of rats, we get rid of garbage trucks and their fumes and noise, we get plants that pump oxygen into the air, we get plants that store carbon and fix nitrogen.' Pérez Rivero is referring to the 'cascade effect', which is central to food planning design. Like a cascade of water down a mountain, the benefits of food initiatives continue to spill over an ever-widening territory. Start with a garden project to improve nutrition, and then let it happen: the benefits of exercise, socializing with neighbors, knowledge about environmental processes, reduction in greenhouse gases, increased safety in parks, a more walkable city, enhanced entrepreneurial skills, heightened interest of tourists...

There are many reasons why Cubans have come this far so fast. They are unusually well educated, which makes it easier to learn and adapt. When I spoke at a 2012 scientific conference on breeding seeds for the looming era of global warming, for example, I learned that this tiny country has 217 science-and-technology centers, 70,000 scientific workers and 110 science journals. There are 67 extension agents in Havana to advise growers, and 220 crop-protection institutes. Secondly, the Cuban state can mandate initiatives, such as delivery of free or low-cost meals at childcare centers, schools, and large workplaces, which guarantee people at least one nutritious meal a day. Though not a democracy, the Cuban government does empower people with skills and knowledge and accepts some level of frank exchange and debate. The level of social capital in the country is astounding. Streets are safe, people are friendly, open and talkative, music adds delight to street scenes, and black-market entrepreneurialism thrives to provide some of the extras of life. Created by a popular revolution, Cuba is peppered with grassroots groups of many kinds, including unions, women's groups and multi-purpose Committees in Defense of the Revolution. Cuba confirms the critical role played by social capital and institutional capacity in facilitating the transition to food security and food sovereignty.[7]

The 'organopónico'

In Alamar, on the outskirts of Havana, a former tree nursery and garbage dump has been turned into a 10-hectare *organopónico* in the midst of a residential neighborhood. The staff of 160 co-op workers is run by Miguel Salcines Lopez and his daughter, Maria Salcines Milla. Neither had farmed before they took charge of the project.

In the space of a hundred-meter walk with Maria, we pass a neem tree, known as a miracle tree in India because of its medicinal leaves, and then I'm shown marigolds, mango, coffee, guava, a clearing for anyone who wants to hold a wedding or anniversary, goats and rabbit huts with roofs made of palm leaves. My hosts pause to tell me that one goal of the project is to change the public image of farm work by providing workers with free breakfast and lunch, free haircuts and time off to take classes. 'The goal is to provide the community with fresh food at a good price because we belong to the community,' she tells me. About 95 per cent of what the *organopónicos* grow is sold in the neighborhood, and the rest goes to Hemingway's, one of the new high-end restaurants in Havana opened up by the entrepreneurs welcomed by Raul Castro. We use food production as a way to teach people and as a community-building activity, Salcines Milla says.

On we go. I see rows of mushrooms under netting and sites for turmeric and other medicinal plants, which the government sees as having export potential. A large clearing is for sugar cane raised for people and livestock, then a clump of Moringa bushes rich in Vitamin C, protein and fatty acids. I'm told they make 400 tonnes of compost a year and also supply neighbors with fruit trees for their yards.

Then we walk through a few hectares of raised beds of lettuce, bok choy, carrots and herbs. We have reached the main street, where the farmers' market is doing a brisk business with neighbors, and Salcines Milla passes me a tall glass of fresh-squeezed sugar-cane juice – as nutritionally rich as blackstrap molasses, only more delicious. She would offer me a drink for the road, she says, except that they're desperately short of containers. Lack of containers is the most pressing limit on how much we can sell, she says. I'd almost forgotten during this tour that Cuba remains strapped for everyday conveniences and equipment. This is a first world country in terms of education, health services and culture, but not at all when it comes to consumer goods and conveniences.

Building heaven
I get back to the scientific conference just in time to meet Fernando Funes-Monzote, the leading Cuban promoter

of agro-ecological strategies to grow resilient systems that can adapt to climate change. Before I know it, I've been invited to tour the family farm he's been working for the past year.

The farm is in an area of long-abandoned sugar-cane plantations that surround Havana. Unable to meet world price points for sugar, the government shut them down and distributed more than a million hectares to 100,000 smallhold farmers and co-ops.

It's a rough and ready farm, but agro-ecology methods can roll with the punches. Wild bamboo from an area near a creek that runs through the property is used for fencing and outdoor furniture. Funes-Monzote has built one section of fencing with small flowering bushes to attract bees. He hopes to sell the dark honey for two dollars a bottle in Havana, while the government hopes the honey can be an export crop. We stroll by an area he's planted with 500 coffee trees, and a few palm trees that produce fruit loved by pigs. Trees are preferred to annuals because the land then doesn't require ploughing each year, which is good for storing carbon and preventing erosion. The palms also remind us that pigs were once forest animals, and don't have to be fed a steady diet of corn out of a trough. The palm can also adapt to his farm's low-quality soil, though he adds that 'there are no bad soils, just badly used soils.' Funes-Monzote is also partial to trees because they live a long life. His PhD thesis was titled 'Farming as if we were here to stay'. Sustainability is built into his design, not added on as an afterthought.

I'm shown coconut trees that shade sweet potato, corn, tomatoes and cassava, which are not far from the barley and sorghum for the chickens. 'There is no threshold for the use of resources or diversity,' Funes-Monzote says, because each species creates food for another species, as well as for the farmer who does the design work. 'I started with 3 chickens and now I have 30,' he says. He hopes to add sheep, bees, rabbits and turkeys to the mix, each of which will add something.

We're soon back at the cabin where his family lives, with soccer goalposts in front, where his two boys are playing. A friend takes a machete to a coconut to lop off the top, and offers me a drink of coconut water, right out of the coconut. Funes-Monzote sees my pleasure. 'You can build heaven,' he says.

Brazil and the Zero Hunger Campaign

People in Brazil's *Zero Fome* (Zero Hunger) movement use very different words from people working with Cuba's gardening revolution. Empowerment, inclusion, ethics, citizenship, civil society, base organization, capacity building, rights, duties – these are words that cropped up when Brazil's anti-hunger campaign was launched in 2004. More ambitious than the UN's goal to reduce world hunger by half, Brazil's campaign commits the country to freeing almost 40 million people – a fifth of the population in the world's sixth biggest economy – from hunger within a decade.

I and four other Torontonians are among a small group of foreigners invited to the campaign launch, an expression of thanks to our city for welcoming Herbert (Betinho) de Sousa during the 1970s, after he was exiled by military dictators in both Chile and his native Brazil. De Sousa returned to Brazil and led a campaign that is credited with inspiring the government's Zero Hunger commitment. Barely a word is said at the conference about nutrition, gardening, compost or fossil fuels. Instead, the word on everyone's lips is 'empowerment'.

'I never used the word empowerment before 1997,' my traveling companion Debbie Field tells me, as we take a cab to the conference center named after de Sousa and an earlier anti-hunger crusader. Field opens a photo album, and shows me pictures of women she met during a 1997 trip to Brazil. The women had just built their homes with bricks they made in a hand-operated machine that de Sousa bought with donations from a nearby synagogue. 'He believed in us, so we believed in ourselves, and look what we did for ourselves,' the women told Field.

'That was Betinho's gift,' Field told me. He made people proud enough to 'do things for themselves, without waiting for government to get its act together, but still seeing the need for government action'. Whether in Toronto or Brazil, Betinho taught that 'social movements should be about ethics, solidarity, transparency and citizenship' and that 'citizenship is a two-way street, not just about government doing things for people,' Field said.

Suddenly, the cab driver screeches to a stop, turns around, and grabs Field's arm. 'You knew Betinho!' he shouts, 'You knew Betinho!' The nickname Betinho means 'little guy', a reference to de Sousa being short and slight. By this name is he loved and cherished to this day, many years after his death. 'This tiny man with giant charisma lifted a nation's hopes, and became the collective metaphor of an aroused Brazilian democracy,' is how one of his first Toronto friends, Judy Hellman, puts it.

When the Brazilian dictatorship stepped down in 1979, Betinho came home. He quickly organized IBASE (the Brazilian Institute for Social and Economic Analysis), one of the first independent organizations in democratic Brazil. A hemophiliac, he contracted AIDS from a blood transfusion in 1985. In 1986, he founded one of the world's premier organizations confronting AIDS. In 1993, he started Citizens' Action against Hunger and Poverty and For Life. Its slogan was 'Hunger Can't Wait'. The organization quickly won backing from a thousand civil-society organizations, and set up 5,000 action committees. To speed up implementation, Betinho launched the Committee of Public Enterprises to Fight Hunger. In 1993, it enlisted 33 public firms and universities to donate surplus materials for creating hundreds of brick-making machines, fish farms and urban gardens, and to become customers of newly formed worker co-ops.

'A rich diversity of direct, local, self-help, independent and grassroots engagement comes from the bottom-up nature of social movements in Brazil,' says Jaime Kirzner-Roberts, a Latin American specialist at Princeton University. 'It's a gut reaction and article of faith among those who've suffered so long from the concentration of power around a tiny economic and government élite,' she says. Popular organizations in Brazil have long known to spread their wings and extend their power base beyond the state, she says.

Lines of action in Belo Horizonte

Belo Horizonte is an industrial city home to three million people, a third of whom live in poverty. It is the leading success story of municipal human rights-based programs against hunger. Since Patrus Ananias of the Workers' Party won the mayoralty in 1993, hunger levels have gone down. The center of the action is the city's Secretariat of Supplies, because Mayor Ananias wanted the lead department to focus on delivering the goods. All people have a right to adequate amounts of quality food, he said, and 'it is the duty of governments to guarantee this right'.

Compare his focus on service delivery with what the UN asks of national governments. In 1999, the UN adopted General Comment 12, a guide to categories of action that national governments can follow to honor their food obligations. The list starts with 'Respect', upholding the access people already have – respecting gardening as a legitimate use of green space in cities, for example. The list moves on to 'Protect', using government powers to keep anyone from taking away existing access to food – preventing a beach resort from keeping villagers from fishing along the beach, for example. The list proceeds to 'Fulfill, Part 1', facilitating access to food – organizing community gardens, for example. The list ends with 'Fulfill, Part 2', actually providing food to people in dire need – after a hurricane or flood, for example. No matter how strapped for money a government is, it can start on at least one front, and gradually move to higher levels, the General Comment suggests.[8]

When I was working on Toronto's Food and Hunger Action Plan, we came up with a similar grid, adapted to the limited financial and decision-making abilities of most city governments. Start with 'Advocate': the mayor can pressure a senior level of government to improve school meals, for instance. Move on to 'Co-ordinate': city staff can help citizens organize a farmers' market at City Hall, for example. Carry on with 'Support': city staff can offer park space and equipment to help a neighborhood group start a community garden, for instance. Then proceed to 'Innovate': adopt incentives for green roofs where food can be grown, for example. Both the UN and the City of Toronto guidelines avoid a showdown over inevitably big budget programs focused on buying and donating food to people who are hungry. Both guidelines cut a lot of slack for the 'neoliberal' approach to government that has held sway internationally since the 1990s – the view that government's job is to steer the boat, not actually to row it.

But that's not the approach of former Mayor Ananias. I met him many years later when he toured Toronto as a senior cabinet minister of the national government. Wearing a blue business suit, he toured FoodShare, which promotes citizen initiatives for food security, and was shown the bins used for community composting. Blue suit and white shirt be damned, he just walked up to the bin, stuck his arm in the pile, and took a whiff. It was the same when he was elected mayor of Belo Horizonte. He started with three 'lines of action', all requiring direct government action. In my experience, anyone moving to direct action on hunger, however progressive or conservative the rationale, is way ahead of the curve.[9]

The 'first line of action' in Belo Horizonte served

people suffering malnutrition. As an emergency measure, pregnant and nursing moms received nutrient-rich 'flour' made of wheat flour, corn flour, wheat bran, ground eggshells and powder from manioc leaves. Since then, meals for children at schools or city-run childcare centers qualify as first-line assistance. The city's sanitation department picks up unsold food at farmers' markets at the end of a day, then cleans and vacuum-packs it for delivery to neighborhood organizations serving members on a low income – a measure designed to provide food to people at risk of hunger, but one that rewards people who participate in community activities that can help them overcome the isolation and despair of poverty. A city-sponsored food bank does the same with donations from supermarkets.

The 'second line of action' helps businesses respond to the needs of people on low incomes. Four medium-sized 'popular restaurants' are supported by the city. They are open for lunch and dinner on workdays. Meals are simple but nutritious – rice, beans, salad and fruit are typical. All customers pay the same subsidized rate. Customers include workers, students, homeless youth, street vendors and seniors. Again using food as an opportunity to build personal skills and sense of social entitlements, regular customers of the 'popular restaurants' can join an organization to lobby for improvements. Also on the list for second line of action are 4,000 modestly subsidized 'popular food baskets', with about 20 food basics. A list of prices at stores across the city is widely circulated, helping people use their food dollars well. These second-line programs are carefully designed to be universal, rather than exclusively targeting a particular vulnerable group. Anyone from any walk of life can benefit from a popular restaurant or list of budget food outlets, for example, even though the service is most needed by people on low incomes, and there is no stigma attached to making use of the service, thus breaking the 'vicious circle of poverty' by fostering inclusion at every opportunity.

Belo Horizonte's 'third line of action' works on 'incentives to basic food production' that lead to actual redesign of the food system. One program helps transport local farmers' fresh produce to the city and subsidizes farmers who provide well-priced foods at farmers' markets in low-income neighborhoods. This is a four-way win for food security. It raises the incomes of small farmers, helping them overcome hunger. It helps small farmers stay on the land instead of swelling the numbers of people seeking jobs in the city. It increases the availability of nutritious foods, since large farms in Brazil are typically dedicated to the export of sugar and oilseeds, leaving small farmers to handle fruit and vegetables for the domestic market. Fourth, by increasing supply, the price of produce is kept stable. In another third line of action, the city orders local produce for 155,000 meals a day in popular restaurants and schools. Still another innovative third-line-of-action project has city staff teaching backyard gardening and artisanal food preparation to help residents become self-employed or self-sufficient. Little wonder that Belo Horizonte has the highest consumption of fruit and vegetables in Brazil.[10]

Whatever the specific program or line of action, all services are designed around enhancing personal skills and social connections and around preventing a passive or fatalistic 'culture of poverty' from taking hold of someone momentarily down on their luck. For example, emergency meals for pregnant or breastfeeding moms ensure that the next generation is born without irreversible physical, psychological or mental handicaps that are caused by malnutrition.

Bolsa Familia – welfare that works

The Zero Hunger campaign is national. National government initiatives are based on ongoing consultations and consensus-building with citizen anti-hunger groups.

They are adequately funded and very smartly planned. Former President Lula served as figurehead for the campaign, speaking passionately about his youth as a poor shoeshine boy who often went hungry.

The flagship program is 'Bolsa Familia', a family allowance program created in 2003 that puts about four billion dollars a year – about one per cent of the national government's budget – into the hands of moms who will use it to feed their children so they do well at school. Arguably the most generous income-transfer program in the Global South, Bolsa Familia wins regular raves from the likes of the neoliberal magazine *The Economist*. In 2013, World Bank Alternate Executive Director Rogerio Studart praised the program for breaking the cycle of poverty by promoting health and education.[11] By 2011, 26 per cent of the population (50 million people), were covered by the program.[12] Bolsa Familia is commonly referred to as a 'conditional transfer', meaning that the money is treated almost as a fee in return for certain services. Pregnant and breastfeeding moms are expected to consult a doctor and follow medical recommendations on nutrition and related matters, so that their child makes a good start in life. Moms of young children are expected to make sure their children, especially their daughters, attend school, rather than keeping them at home to help with household chores. An anti-poverty program triples the value of an equitable social program by also contributing to health and educational programs that result in public savings.

Some label the program conditional, as distinct from an entitlement program that has no behavioral expectation – such as a retirement pension that automatically goes to people over 65, just because they are citizens. I consider Bolsa Familia an entitlement program for children and mothers, because it ensures the money goes to and for them. As a kid, I knew my mom received a monthly 'mother's allowance' to cover the costs of each child because some shrewd if patronizing government officials suspected that if the extra money went to men, it might end up being spent in a pub. Bolsa Familia likely draws on this tradition. I believe it's consistent with the views of Olivier De Schutter, a distinguished UN advocate on the right to food, who says that strengthening 'women's rights is the secret weapon against hunger', and 'is the single most effective step to realizing the right to food' and ending the cycle of inherited poverty.[13]

Bolsa Familia funds go directly from the national government to the bank accounts of families living in poverty, with no bureaucracy or expenses in between – an important point for the governing Workers Party, which fears bureaucratic inertia and is intent on breaking up patronage relationships between local powerbrokers and high-needs individuals – the 'you scratch my back, I'll scratch yours' syndrome of relationships that often undermines political independence of pauperized communities 'obligated' to some local strongman. The success of Bolsa Familia led the national government to bankroll a similar program for indigenous peoples in the Amazon, who receive funding in return for efforts contributing to environmental protection.

The national government astutely folds food-related funding into programs that don't explicitly have a food mandate, thereby taking full advantage of the gateway or leveraging potential of food. Nationally funded school meals, for example, provide a major daily meal to 36 million children in regional development programs in low-income areas of north and northeast Brazil. Food purchases for school meals go to small farms, where 77 per cent of agrarian workers are employed. Other anti-poverty programs with food and agriculture implications include the $5 billion spent to help settle over 350,000 landless farm families on idle farm parcels owned by rich landowners.[14] An infrastructure program called 'Territories of Citizenship' puts $6.4 billion into schools, clinics and electric utilities in about a thousand relatively isolated towns in 60 areas identified by the UN as at-risk for poverty and ill-health.[15]

The buoyant economy that has allowed the government to sustain this level of support for nutrition, food security and anti-poverty programs is to some extent based on good luck as much as good planning. Brazil is well-endowed with natural resources – water, agricultural land and mineral wealth, including oil. Chinese and European demand for various products, including soy (much of it genetically engineered), keeps both investment and revenue coming into the economy. As a result, some of the benefits of Brazil's food-security programs are offset by environmental losses and by long-term subordination to powerful agribusiness interests that have invested heavily in the country's rich and aggressive export-oriented agricultural sector, mainly to provide low-cost meat to Europe and China.[16] The integrity of the Amazon rainforest may end up being sacrificed to the export-oriented and megaproject focus of many economic development projects.

Just as Cuba's lack of political democracy modifies any praise for government and NGO anti-hunger achievements in the areas of food security and food sovereignty, so Brazil's inability to restrain carnivorous agribusiness leaves a bad aftertaste on any full assessment of sustainable food systems. Nevertheless, I can't but respect what they have done to reduce hunger.

Yorito, Honduras

The most intriguing municipal politician I've met in my food travels is Maryin Gonzales, Mayor of Yorito, which is the name for both a township and a village with a total population of 20,000 mostly indigenous people in the ruggedly beautiful mountains of Honduras. Yorito is definitely off the beaten track. The village has dirt roads and open ditches, and its first public restaurant opened in the fall of 2012 when I visited. Stray dogs, chickens and pigs have the run of the road. Early in the morning, men can be seen heading off to a plantation holding their machete in one hand and the reins of a donkey in the other. As elsewhere in Honduras, two-thirds of the people live in poverty, half live in extreme poverty, 22 per cent of women of child-bearing age die during childbirth, and about half of all newborns die in infancy.

Gonzales is a rancher, and wears blue jeans, cowboy boots and a large silver heart on a chain around her neck. She is larger than life. Did I mention she packs a pistol in an open holster? When she heard I worked for a city on food issues, she asked me to meet at her office.

Her desk is dominated by crafts from Yorito artisans. There are purses made of pop bottle caps by local women, woodworking by high-school teens and bottled water from a local co-op filtration plant. Yorito supports these artisans as part of an anti-poverty economic development plan, she says. The township invests if there's a good business plan and is paid back with interest if the business succeeds, and thereby becomes a revolving fund for business start-ups. She wants to find someone to set up artisanal food businesses producing local products that compete with pop and potato chips.

Gonzalez shifts the topic to her big campaign, which is to reduce infant mortality. She tells me what she does with a total budget of about two million dollars covering housing, sewage, a new farmers' market building, economic development and food.

She rolls food in with housing initiatives. You have to be holistic, she tells me. For instance, when houses are in bad repair, babies are exposed to more infectious diseases. So the township helped with 370 home renovations that upgraded household sanitation, especially as it relates to food. Homes are also where people can garden and grow their own food. The township helped 400 families start home gardens, where avocado, squash and chickens could be raised. There is a class on keeping homes with newborns ultra-clean. In addition, there is support for people who set up sanitary latrines. The mayor evidently does not believe in silos, one for food and one for housing. Few subjects interact more dynamically than food and housing. People who don't see that connection think people who can't afford food need help with food, when really they need help with rent, which takes the money they need to spend on food. There aren't many townships in the world that understand this relationship.

Children go to school, so the mayor works with schools to get food to children, again oblivious to the fact that food and education are normally in two totally different silos of governments. There's a program to pay local dairy farmers to deliver fresh milk daily to provide every student with at least one glass of milk. Every school must have a garden so that children can sample the food and learn how to grow it at home. People on low incomes, as in less than two dollars a day, need to economize when they shop. So the township has a storage facility for people who buy food in season when the price is lowest. People with young children need a way to learn about best practices together. The township pays for classes on home hygiene and on cooking for infants under two. There are also courses on bookkeeping for farmers.

To make more fresh food available, the township paid for a building to house a farmers' market. Part of its appeal is that it will keep local money in the local economy, and encourage farmers to grow a little surplus for sale.

Yorito engages the local population through nine community councils, including ones focused on agriculture, health, coffee, livestock, and cultural projects to recover indigenous heritage. To attract know-how, connections and other resources, the township partners with 12 groups, including the FAO and the Catholic Church.

Of course, the resources brought to bear in this

township can't compare to what is happening in Brazil and Cuba. That is the point. Mayor Gonzalez's favorite saying is 'push the cart forward'. In a country marred by a recent coup and political assassinations, where the best lands in the valley have been seized from indigenous peoples on behalf of agriculture that is focused on exports, there's an opportunity to push the cart forward. The formula is amenable to any community of any size. Pick achievable targets, which engage people dealing with hunger in pushing the cart. Identify areas of overlap – in this case housing, employment, education and increased sales of local food – that bring more reasons and more people to push the cart. Engage the community and partners with broad projects that provide space for partnerships and overlapping benefits.

From political will to agency

There are, to be sure, many other uplifting examples of programs promoting access to good food for all. But the key points illustrated here will likely be confirmed by them. Cuba, Brazil and the little township of Yorito show the importance of going beyond political will to agency – the confidence and competence to advocate for and manage the effective delivery of food programs. Agency is empowerment matched by know-how and effectiveness. Fostering such agency, in my view, should become the centerpiece for food-system advocates.

At the 2004 Zero Hunger conference I attended, former Belo Horizonte Mayor Ananias, in his new position as Minister for Social Development and Hunger Alleviation, told a thousand people that social justice and personal ethical development are 'the greatest goals we have' – a formulation that expresses the inspiration of Roman Catholic liberation theology (a belief that working for social justice is doing Christ's work) among Brazilian food activists. We 'need to have popular democracy in place where citizens have rights and duties,' as well as 'social control over the state' and 'autonomy of social movements,' Ananias said, 'as in Belo Horizonte.' This formulation expresses a strong commitment to robust citizen organizations and to what University of Toronto sociologist Harriet Friedmann has called 'communities of food practice'.[17] The centrality of such grassroots capacity is one reason why municipal governments, historically closest to community groups, need to be identified as major government actors and delivery vehicles in food-security programming.

I'm also impressed by the intuitive grasp Cuban, Brazilian and Yorito leaders have for programs, not just policies. Brazil and Cuba, in sharp contrast to many jurisdictions, had the capacity and knack to develop programs with goals, deliverables, budget lines, staff, and partnerships – the works. Food programming with the works puts food on the table. Belo Horizonte put its top-priority food programs in the trust of the most humble department of a city, Supplies, because the mayor wanted to deliver supplies and services to people who had rights. Such humility and commitment to serve people – in some managerial circles it's called servant leadership – at some point become pivotal to success. These will be hallmarks of a food system that transcends the current model of industrial food resting on the sale of commodities.

1 World Food Programme, 'Fighting Hunger Worldwide: Hunger is the world's greatest solvable problem'. **2** FAO, *The State of Food Insecurity in the World, 2005,* pp 2-5. **3** FAO, *The State of Food Insecurity in the World 2006* pp 4, 7. **4** www.globalissues.org, Food Aid. **5** A Sen, *Development and Freedom*, Random House, 1999, pp 162-180; J Druze and A Sen, *Hunger and Public Action*, Oxford, 2006. **6** M Altieri, F Funes-Monzote, 'The Paradox of Cuban Agriculture,' *Monthly Review*, Jan 2012, is rich in statistics. **7** For two excellent references, see F Funes et al, *Sustainable Agriculture and Resistance*, Food First, 2002, and M Cruz and R Medina, *Agriculture in the City*, IDRC 2001. **8** United Nations, Economic and Social Council, Committee on Economic, Social and Cultural Rights, *General Comment 12*: Geneva: ECOSOC E/C.12/1999/5. **9** City of Toronto, Food and Hunger Action Committee, *Planting the Seeds* (2000) and *The Growing Season* (2001). **10** Cecilia Rocha, 'Urban Food Security Policy: The Case of Belo Horizonte, Brazil,' *Journal for the Study of Food and Society*, 5, 1, Summer 2001, pp 36-47; C Rocha and Adriana Aranha, 'Urban Food Policies and Rural

Bread and roses

Sustainability – How the Municipal Government of Belo Horizonte, Brazil is promoting Rural Sustainability', unpublished paper. **11** R Studart, 'Brazil and the Global Battle to Eliminate Extreme Poverty,' *The Globalist*, 26 Mar 2013. **12** http://tinyurl.com/czkd9ad **13** O De Schutter, 'Gender and the Right to Food', Report presented to the 22nd Session of the United Nations Human Rights Council, 3 Apr 2013. **14** C Rocha, 'Update from Brazil: Advancing food and nutrition security under the Lula government,' presentation to Canadian Association of Food Studies annual conference, Saskatoon, 2007; J Pedro Stedile, 'The Class Struggle in Brazil: The Perspective of the MST,' *Socialist Register*, 2008; L Panitch and C Leys, eds, *Socialist Register: Global Flashpoints: Reactions to Imperialism and Neoliberalism*, Merlin Ross, 2008. **15** 'Brazil unveils anti-poverty drive,' *BBC News*, 26 Feb 2008, 'Brazil unveils $6.4 billion poverty plan,' *International Herald Tribune*, 25 Feb 2008. **16** *The Economist*, 'Dreaming of glory: a special report on Brazil,' 14 Apr 2007, pp 12, 14. **17** H Friedmann, 'Scaling up: Bringing public institutions and food service corporations into the project for a local, sustainable food system in Ontario,' in *Agriculture and Human Values*, 24:3, 2007.

6 Seeds of hope: the rise of the food movement

Farmers, corporations, governments and shoppers have long had their say about food. Now there's a new group that wants to be heard. It calls itself the food movement. In its short history, the food movement has already become a major contender for influence around the world. This last chapter reviews the challenges it raises and faces.

MANY PEOPLE come to the food movement looking for a hopeful place to stand and a joyous place to start. But even foodies sing the blues. The atmosphere has passed the milestone 400 parts per million of carbon, which likely means severely negative and long-term havoc in the climate affecting food production. Major fisheries, the source of lean protein, healthy fats and brain food, are at death's door. And so on. But the thing to remember is that the bigger the problems, the more food can do.

One of the inviting things about food is its capacity for positive impact. This works in at least two ways. If I switch from low-quality coffee, I likely go from beans raised on a plantation with damaging impact on wild birds to beans raised in forests with positive impact on wild birds. It's like going from minus 2 to plus 2, which means the point spread of impact from one tiny action adds up to 4. Actually, it gets better. The pattern with food is that if it's good for one aspect of life, it will be good for other aspects. The coffee that's good for wildlife because it's not sprayed with toxic pesticides is also safer for workers. When producers grow without synthetic pesticides, they save money on inputs. With fair-trade products, a portion of the premium must go to community projects such as schools, so the whole community benefits. The positive ripple effect extends from wildlife protection to worker health to business viability to community improvement. What started as a 4-point spread, ends up as a 16-point spread from such as modest choice as buying fair-trade coffee or cocoa.

The other nice thing is that farming to a different drummer actually works. We CAN feed and nourish the world. Jules Pretty, a sustainable-agriculture expert from Essex University in England, worked up the hard numbers. His 2001 study, *Reducing Food Poverty with Sustainable Agriculture: A Summary of New Evidence*, reviews 208 innovative farm projects by nine million farmers in 28 countries. In 10 years, impoverished farmers jacked up the amount of land under earth-friendly stewardship by an astounding 28,000 per cent, from 100,000 to 29,000,000 hectares. The greatest increase in farm productivity came from small farms working to increase a 'sustainability dividend' by paying attention to 'natural' and 'social' capital – improvements to the environment and community.

When fish are raised in rice paddies, Pretty discovered, there's a health, environmental and economic dividend. The fish eat insects that might otherwise spread malaria. The fish also enrich the soil with their excrement. Then they provide a protein-rich meal to the farmers. Productivity comes from designing virtuous circles, he found.

In 2007, two reports added heft to these findings. At an FAO conference in 2007, Dadia El-Hage Scialabba highlighted the relevance of organic methods to farmers with limited resources. Conventional methods may produce higher yields, she said, but smallholder farmers can't afford the expensive hybrid seeds, fertilizers, and so on, and lack access to a market to sell any surplus produce. Organic methods require labor rather than cash, and are therefore more affordable, she said. Ability to make use of local, low-cost and natural assets such as animal manure is 'the strongest feature of organic agriculture', Scialabba claimed. Later that year, Ivette Perfecto from the University of Michigan reviewed 293 case studies, which showed that organic methods can yield over 2,641 calories per person per day.[1]

Here's an example of evidence rolling in every day. In the tiny village of Darveshpura in Bihar, India's poorest state, a smallholder farmer named Sumant Kumar grew 22.4 tonnes of rice on one hectare of land. His world record was achieved without any genetically engineered seeds, commercial fertilizers or pesticides, and without any help from agricultural researchers. When Sumant's friend Nitish beat the world record for potato yields and a farmer from a nearby village did the same for wheat, the threesome won attention as miracle workers. On the surface, Kumar's technique is simple – apply composted manure to the soil and plant the rice seedlings 25 centimeters apart in dry land – a labor-intensive method which represents a huge shift from transplanting several seedlings close together in land that's been flooded by water. Kumar's method, known as System of Rice Intensification (SRI), was developed during the 1980s by a French priest, Henri de Laulanie, working in Madagascar, and has been promoted since by Cornell University researcher Norman Uphoff. The beauty of the method is that it boosts yields while reducing water use and avoiding the methane produced when rice grows under water. For Uphoff, it makes a beautiful point – that the key to advancing productivity does not lie in labs where scientists manipulate miracle genes, but in the soil, where farmers create fertility with natural materials.[2]

Just as water simmers and then suddenly breaks into a boil and changes state to steam, today's good food movement is simmering with individual projects such as I've just summarized, and is getting ready to let off steam with transformational ones. Transformational projects, according to Toronto scholar Charles Levkoe, have three qualities. They aim for scaled-up community-wide participation, they get people thinking about food systems, and they go beyond such 'safe' issues as local and nutritious to take up bracing challenges of sustainability.[3] They produce tipping points. Coming soon to a community near you: community food centers, hubs, school gardens that are part of a food curriculum, food studies programs at universities, year-round farmers' markets, community gardens in every park, green roofs on every institutional building and high-rise, local and sustainable meals in hospitals and schools, food policy councils…

Food movement leaders increasingly promote personal skills and habits and community 'capacity' and 'assets' that can transform. Community gardens, community kitchens, neighborhood farmers' markets, forest gardens and community baking ovens are intuitive first projects. They all pose the issue of food belonging in the community, or the 'commons'. The close-to-home approach of recovering informal public space led food organizers to focus attention on city governments, despite the fact they have no formal jurisdiction over food issues.

Two Toronto organizations, FoodShare (I'm a member of its board) and The Stop represent best practice in this area. FoodShare runs an 'animator program' that breathes life into social-housing projects reducing the impact of poverty with community gardens, kitchens and community fresh-food markets. Leaders at The Stop just started a national campaign to make community food centers the 21st-century equivalent of neighborhood libraries, parks and recreation centers. Such programs recognize the whole-of-society support systems needed to complement individual efforts. Social connections have to be consciously cultivated, not left to chance. The neighborhood is where food strategy starts to unfold. That's the theme of Toronto's Food Strategy of 2010, which I helped draft.

Truth be told, government laws, support and subsidies are also essential to whatever food system prevails. Free-market systems for food are a figment of the imagination. Today's dominant food system would fall apart in short order if it were not propped up by laws and direct and indirect subsidies, and the emerging alternative food system will be no different.

Most people active in food movements believe governments must break free from a one-silo approach – usually controlled by a department of agriculture – and engage people from all departments that touch on food – most obviously departments of health and environment, but also community development, rural affairs, transportation, waste management, economic development and education. Whole-of-government perspectives and delivery mechanisms are a precondition for any government hoping to play a positive role in food system improvement. Food councils, such as I worked for, are a first step in that direction.

The origins of today's food movement

The ingredients needed to cook up a storm with a global food movement came together in the 1990s. The internet came into its own at the same time. This is not a coincidence. Networks are better at herding cats than disciplined groupings, so food types, as manageable as cats, took full advantage of internet applications that allow loose networks to handle such core organizing functions as information sharing, advocacy and collaboration on specific projects. The biggest forces on the internet, such as Google and Facebook, were also models for movement organizing, in that their business consists of offering platforms that connect people. The Occupy movement of 2011 famously adapted this platform model, but the food movement took to it naturally because food itself comes from a worldwide web in which convening people is second nature. This can be seen in the way food brings people together at weddings, wakes, political banquets, Valentine's dinners, Christmas feasts, fundraisers and birthday parties, without specifying formal points of programmatic agreement.[4]

Seeds of hope

The 1990s were also defined by the collapse of the Soviet Union and the formal end to the Cold War. This created space for a new ideologically unaffiliated force to emerge around food, which did not fit on the rigid left or right. Many of the 'welfare state' measures that came out of the early years of the Cold War during the late 1940s were dismantled then. On the one hand, that led to an increase of inequality and poverty, which put hunger and food insecurity high up on the food movement's to-do list. On the other, the dissolution of welfare-state programs left a vacuum filled by non-profits and non-governmental organizations (NGOs), which have mushroomed in the food sector and proven to be beachheads of expertise and advocacy for food-related causes. It is unlikely that any government agency can match NGOs for depth of knowledge or experience in food – a huge leg up for the food movement and part of the reason why its media profile has been so high.

People from the Global South play leading roles in the food movement, thereby turning traditional colonial-era North-South relations right-side up. People in the Global South formed La Via Campesina, the largest general food and agriculture organization in the world. In addition, Global South practices inspired many innovations coming out of the global food movement – community kitchens, community bake ovens, farmers' markets, seed exchanges, street vending, food trucks, urban agriculture and gardening in vacant public spaces. Critics of the food movement in the Global North commonly refer to such practices as élitist, which may amuse those who developed these survival techniques of impoverished peoples, who knew to compensate for lack of money with richness of informal community.

Connecting the world
Making connections and getting things done are two of the hallmarks of today's food movement.[5] We are a movement of 'ands', not 'buts', says Vandana Shiva,

a food-movement superstar from India. 'We are about propositionists, not oppositionists', says FoodShare's Debbie Field.

The food movement has many different types of connectors. In addition to the campaigners, there are social entrepreneurs, who delight in turning a problem into an opportunity that serves the public interest while generating an income. Michael Sacco of Toronto- and Oaxaca-based ChocoSol, which sells directly traded artisanal chocolate, is a social entrepreneur who describes himself as an 'actionist,' someone who embodies his ideals in his work and life, not an activist who pressures governments to change laws. Another food connector is the broker, who works to put the bug of a Big Idea in some influential person's ear. Food also has its share of policy wonks who love weaving ideas. There are also artisans, who love to express themselves through their hands at a high level of excellence – the people who become chefs, bakers and graphic artists for the movement. Last but not least are the joie de vivrists, who have lots of love and joy to share, and who find their voice in community food projects.

The connection theme resonates throughout the Global South. Agro-ecology thrives in the Global South by connecting all the allied needs met by growing and collecting fruits, leaves for thatched roofs and lumber for home construction in heavily treed areas interspersed with annual crops. In areas of Africa where outsiders have yet to establish plantations, forests outside villages 'act as grocery store, pharmacy and hardware store rolled into one', as people carry on historic cultures connecting needs for food, medicine, crafts, firewood, dyes, chemicals, livestock and art materials, says journalist Joan Baxter. Coffee and cacao growers in Central America organize co-ops that connect directly with Northern supporters so farmers can also enjoy a cup of hope by capturing more of the value of quality coffee and chocolate. In Japan, a teikei or relationship-based food system based on co-ops, direct trade and trust helped people weather the double trauma of a tsunami and nuclear-plant breakdown without panicking about food availability, access or safety.

London calling

Jeanette Longfield co-ordinates London-based Sustain: The alliance for better food and farming, which represents about 100 public-interest organizations in the UK connected to food and agriculture. Longfield personifies the food movement connector. She played a key role brokering citizen input into London's food strategy of 2006, which came with a 10-year plan and $8-million budget to increase local, healthy, safe, sustainable and universally accessible food in one of the world's great cities. 'Getting it going, moving networks into action, is more important than getting it right,' she says.

The first job is to 'change the conversation' by connecting with the needs of key groups that must be onside. Mayors, for example, relate more to food as a tourist attraction, or as jobs for at-risk youth, or as a way to revitalize streets – issues that mayors are held to account on – than they relate to nutrition, which is not their mandate. So Longfield calls food a 'latchkey issue' which unlocks a multi-purpose strategy to boost local jobs, raise the profile of local restaurants, reduce pollution from long-distance transportation, protect nearby farmers and farmland, and improve food access for people on low incomes.[6]

Having broken the ice with her core sponsors, Longfield proceeds to stage two connections: 'bridge the divides'. That's a tall order in the food sector, thanks to a history of farmers feeling insulted by environmentalists, people on low incomes feeling put down by 'yuppie foodies', and so on. Overcoming these disconnects of the past is essential, because politicians won't touch a project that could blow up into bitter infighting.

Longfield then moves to stage three connections: 'rebuilding the middle'. It's taken me many years to realize just how far-seeing she was to name this a next-step issue in 2006. Today's food leaders are excited about one approach to rebuilding the middle called 'hubs', as in the hub of a bike wheel, with spokes going in many directions but all making a stronger wheel. Hubs will be to the food movement what trains, container ships, tractor trailers, freeways and giant warehouses have been to the long-distance food system. That infrastructure overcame physical distance, but replaced it with social, psychological, cultural and dietary distance from food. Rebuilding the middle will reduce physical, social, cultural and psychological distance.

Rebuilding the middle requires hard infrastructure (freezers and canning facilities, for example) as well as soft infrastructure (meeting places and website designers, for example), and be open to all producers and consumers. One function of such spaces may be to humanize the food system. The modernist food system assumed food was first and foremost a commodity produced for sale, not a service that businesses had to be paid for but which served the public good, as doctors are in most health systems and education consultants are in school systems. Humanizing the food system through local and sustainable infrastructure goes beyond the physical objective of moving food 'from farm to table'. It also introduces people to each other as people, not sellers or buyers. Aside from filling stomachs, togetherness has been a critical function of food since early humans first started to bring food back to a common place to cook and share it. Hubs tap into this human connection as well.

Longfield and her colleagues organized themselves into work crews, one of which instituted a 'race to the top' among separate London boroughs lagging behind in food commitments that had to be delivered before the 2012 Olympics. Sustain galvanized the London food community to work with all levels of government and thousands of individual Londoners. Together they put on a first-class food show for the 2012 Olympics. Among the city's accomplishments were 2012 new community gardens with 98,000 gardeners, 14 million local and sustainable meals catered to athletes; sustainable fish in major restaurants ('avoid the worst, promote the best, improve the rest' was the slogan), zero-waste management systems for food scraps and other materials, a bevy of local beehives and honey producers, a thousand restaurants featuring high animal-welfare standards, and on and on.[7]

The ability to make connections has been a key to Sustain's success in London. Elsewhere in the Global North, one of the most effective connections that food-movement organizations have made is with consumers. The food movement has been clever about harnessing what food writer Michael Pollan calls 'voting with your fork'. At a Toronto after-dinner talk, he made the case that 'food is one of those areas where the personal is the political'. Simple acts such as home cooking of local ingredients from an independent local store can 'help reclaim control of the food system', Pollan said. It's a nice, if rare opportunity 'where the right thing to do is the most delightful thing'.

In the next few pages, I'll present some of the most compelling examples of how the food movement has engaged individual consumers to revive demand for local, ethical, healthy, ecologically responsible and slow foods from backyard and community gardens, farmers' markets and main streets occupied by neighborhood butchers, bakers and candlestick makers. As fans of consumer power turn their attention to scaling up opportunities to create more local and sustainable production, they have set their sights on public-sector purchasing, likely to become a compelling issue of the coming decade.

Boycotts and buycotts

Consumer activists work with two tools. Boycotts try to save the world one bankruptcy at a time. A boycott means voluntarily refusing to purchase a product as an act of protest, with the intention of inflicting economic hardship on the producer of the product. One of the largest consumer boycotts was launched in 1977, and continues to this day, against Nestlé for promoting formula feeding of infants in the Global South, where it is costly and unsafe to use because it must be mixed with water that may be contaminated. Buycotters, by contrast, believe the carrot is better than the stick, and deliberately buy from people going the extra mile to do the right thing. They also see themselves following the maxim often attributed to Gandhi to 'be the change you wish to see'.

Critics of consumer activism argue that activist shoppers simply ape the methods of a consumer culture, so overpowering that even opponents are reduced to new ways of shopping, rather than new expressions of citizenship. Critics also point out that buycotts are a tactic of the affluent, since people on low incomes can't afford more expensive alternatives to cheap food.

However, the critics might note that famous boycotts and buycotts of the past used the positive energy of direct action to develop the economic and political muscle of a developing insurgency. During the Boston Tea Party of 1773, a shipload of tea from the British East India Company was tossed into Boston harbor to protest taxes imposed on American colonists. A buycott of coffee began, followed by the American Revolution a few years later. A few decades after that, Britain's anti-slavery movement, described as the first mass movement of modern times, boycotted slave-grown sugar, then buycotted fair sugar, then succeeded in banning slave labor in the British empire. Likewise, in 1930, Gandhi led his first organized action to bid for India's independence – a march to the ocean to protest British taxes on a local natural resource, salt. The point of Gandhi's campaign was to transform popular consciousness by empowering people to see and act on their right to access their own food commons, the ocean, for their own salt that could not be taxed by the British. Consumer action alone has rarely been the end of a matter, just the beginning.

Organic food

Purchasing organic food has long been a buycott action to support a different form of agriculture. Today, supermarkets and neighborhood 'health food stores' stock a full line of organic drinks, fruits, vegetables, grains and meats, as well as ready-to-serve meals. Organic versions of cosmetics, snack bars and pop tarts have been coming on strong since 2000, along with produce from around the world. The organic 'movement', as it still calls itself, has borne the brunt of angst about youthful idealism lost to the grinding logistics and harsh realities of tough customers who demand unblemished appearances, just-in-time delivery, steady volumes, long shelf life, convenient packaging and low prices.

Organic leaps and bounds

1990: $1 billion in US food and non-food sales
2007: $1.7 billion in US food sales
2008: $3.2 billion in US food sales
2009: 37.2 million hectares in worldwide production
2010: 54 per cent of organic sales in mainstream and mass market outlets
2010: $59.1 billion in global sales
2011: 17,281 certified US farmers, ranchers, processors
2011: $29.2 billion in US food sales
2011: 4.2 per cent of US food sales are organic
2012: $1.3 billion in Australian food sales
2012: $8.4 billion in German sales
2012: $4.7 billion in French sales

Sources: Agricultural Marketing Resource Center; Organic Trade Association.

Some early movement dreams have been compromised, to be sure. But progress has been steady on four fronts. First, brand equity has been built. 'Organic' is a diamond of a word, a shining promise of pastoral purity, natural goodness and wholesome integrity. Second, a steep learning curve has been climbed, and producers have taught themselves to grow, process and sell a full range of good-looking, good-tasting organic foods. Third, the demand for organic options forced mainstream retailers to open their doors to a challenging, high-quality, high-maintenance and premium line of foods that introduced niches to one of the last bastions of mass-production uniformity. Fourth, organics held onto its price premium, a price point that comes close to the real costs of producing foods that respect human and environmental health.

Organic sales came on the mass-retail radar during the 1990s, a decade of internationally profiled food scares – mad cow disease was perhaps the best known – and worrisome innovations, such as genetic engineering. A new constituency of health-minded shoppers in North America and Europe came to organics. The new customers were less attuned to counterculture values, and more concerned about allergies from additives and diseases from toxins. These new organic shoppers didn't know the farmers or processors making their food, and wanted some proof that premium prices were getting them more than good karma. That created pressure for strict certification, and eventually government-backed codes that enjoy consumer respect.

Year after year, organic sales posted double-digit rates of increase, easily the fastest growth rate in the food industry. Organic sales, according to the Organic Trade Association, accounted for 4.2 per cent of US food sales in 2011.[8] This growth has attracted the interest of the mainstream food industry. A number of global food giants have dipped their toes in the pure organic waters by buying out some respected organic companies. General Mills, Kellogg's, Mars, Heinz, Con Agra, ADM, Dole, Danone and Coke can all swing both ways, conventional and organic. As they buy in, the organic 'market segment' begins to duplicate the corporate, long-distance and multi-ingredient supply chain of the conventional system.[9]

To be fair, this trend toward duplication tells us as much about organic customers as about producers. If organic consumers bought only fruits, vegetables, meats and bulk grains and beans, there would be virtually no corporate presence, just as there is virtually no corporate presence at farmers' markets or farm stands. But if organic customers want convenience packaging and non-seasonal foods, they're setting the stage for corporate players. Critics of corporate organic who want to confront system-wide drivers of corporatization should look in the mirror. Organic food needs organic customers who will change their shopping, cooking and eating habits as well as the certification of the food they buy. The two co-evolve, like flowers and bees.

Fair trade

Fair-trade foods and drinks have roared from a standing start in the 1990s to $2 billion in sales by 2006, and $6 billion by 2011. Customers, mostly in the Global North, pay a premium price for coffee, tea, chocolate, dried fruit, bananas and similar products, expecting the premium to go to improved community services and better land stewardship (forest-grown coffee that protects migratory birds' nesting grounds, for example) in the Global South. As many as five million producers in over 30 countries benefit in some way from fair-trade sales. In essence, fair-trade shoppers pay the full price for needs and preferences neglected by cheap food – a delicious, bitter-free cup of coffee, a clear conscience after a treat, and the song of a favorite migratory bird that just flew in from a Global South farm.

As relationships are enriched, the distinction between

fair and far foods may blur. Some fair-trade imports may be seen as 'honorary local' foods, sought out by conscious consumers when there is no locally produced equivalent. The idea that Ethiopia's premium coffees might rate as honorary local foods intrigues Tadesse Meskela, general manager of the 102,000-member Oromia Coffee Farmers' Co-operative Union in south-western Ethiopia, and central figure in *Black Gold*, a gripping documentary about coffee workers.

If defining local food includes intangibles such as connection, quasi-tangibles such as 'terroir', as well as tangibles like embodied energy from field to plate, Meskela thinks his coffee might be considered part of a local food system. That would ease the anxiety of locavores who can't get through a day without several hits of coffee – the second most-traded commodity in the world after oil. It would also relieve people in the Global South who rely on coffee and tea exports because their land (the mountains of Ethiopia, for example) doesn't support many other cash crops. As a general rule, coffee, tea and cacao are crops that meet the needs of the most isolated and marginalized producers who take advantage of the fact that coffee, tea and cacao are non-perishable and high value for their light weight.

Meskela believes that educating coffee consumers will benefit the world's 20 million impoverished coffee growers. He's talking as much about educating the palate as the conscience. Few caffeine addicts know that low-caffeine, sweet and high-quality Arabica coffees such as Sidamo come from Ethiopia, the birthplace of coffee, while the high-caffeine, lower-quality and placeless Robusta coffees were developed to meet the price point of corporate cheap food empires and low-end coffee chains. Robusta jolted the coffee world during the 1990s, when the World Bank encouraged new countries to grow the (until then) decently priced crop, previously raised on bushes along hillsides and mountains. That World Bank initiative swamped world markets with cheap Robusta coffee beans that drove coffee prices into the basement, condemning millions of growers to desperate poverty. On the other side of the coffee glut stood four corporations – Kraft, Nestlé, Procter & Gamble and Sara Lee. Monopolies used their purchasing power to demand prices as low as 40 cents a pound, says Anthony Wild, author of *Coffee, A Dark History*. Fair trade in foods (most products were crafts until that point) were a response to this Bank-sponsored economic tsunami.

Teaching consumers to appreciate the taste, aroma and caffeine levels of Arabica coffee, Meskela hopes they will enjoy a drink that leaves no bitter residue among the people who grew it or the wildlife that cohabit coffee-rich mountains. He tours Europe and North America beating the bushes for community roasters who will partner to promote fresh-roasted coffee from fair-trade Arabica beans. Meskela hopes new relation-ships will keep coffee growers from competing among themselves to sell to four or five global monopolies, and let them focus instead on finding their niche among hundreds of thousands of local roasters who sell fresh, artisan-roasted, naturally low-caffeinated coffee with no bitter aftertaste. Such independent roasters and coffee shops will become anchors of main-street hang-outs and neighborhood employment in the Global North while supporting thousands of prosperous coffee-growing villages.

Under what's called a 'slow trade' regime, green and durable coffee beans can be transported in bulk by ship and train, the least-polluting mode of transportation. That supply chain keeps the money close to where the value is added – growers and roasters. Since 2004, that approach to spreading the wealth has meant five elementary schools, five healthcare centers, 27 water-cleaning facilities, and two construction starts on new high schools in Oromia alone.

'Trade has to work for the poor,' Meskela tells me.

Fair-trade towns

Especially in Britain, activists have stirred flair into their coffee by promoting fair-trade towns and universities. The idea is that large-scale purchases make it easier for individuals to flex their fair-trade economic muscles on a regular basis. Garstang, in Lancashire, was declared the world's first fair-trade town in 2001. By 2007, Britain had 309 fair-trade towns, including London, Aberdeen, Leeds, Bristol and Nottingham. The European Union helps campaigners on the continent, where Rome is the star sign-up. Dutch and Scandinavian cities are joining quickly, as are North American communities. Toronto is set to become the largest fair-trade town in North America.

A fair-trade community makes some practical and achievable commitments. The local council promotes fair trade, and serves fair-trade products at City events. A nominal fee goes to fair-trade co-ops in the developing world. There must be a minimum number of participating retailers and a campaign to increase their numbers. This is the spirit of getting started on 'continuous improvement'.

Malmö, a multicultural city of 270,000 in southern Sweden, shows how businesses, community groups and government agencies co-operate through such participatory democracy methods. Malmö's campaign is led by a church, the Red Cross and a few unions. The Red Cross headquarters, Humanity House, features public exhibitions and talks, as well as a gift shop and café, 'where you can enjoy coffee and a cake with a clear conscience'. Lasting changes must start where people are at, Red Cross leaders explain. A city-funded directory of fair-trade businesses trumpets the consumer's 'power to choose', but notes that 'making an ethical choice is no longer for do-gooders but fashionable and fun'. The directory lists restaurants, gift shops, ice cream, clothing, furniture and grocery stores, as well as chains, discount stores, Pizza Hut and the Hilton. A Swedish-owned fair-trade coffee chain, Barista, is unionized, its owner says, 'because we believe in applying fair trade at home as well'. The city's website encourages tourists to live 'ethically and ecologically in Malmö', with a variety of eco-gourmet tours and green golf courses.

Fair to the Last Drop, a 2007 study by Food First, calls such stepped-up versions of fair trade 'solidarity consumerism'. Such initiatives rely on what public-health experts call 'nudge' or 'environmental support', the kind of social marketing pioneered by anti-smoking advocates, but readily adaptable to food and drink. The idea is to encourage wise purchasing decisions by making them easier and more appealing.[10]

There's no need to wring hands about long-distance imports while sipping fair-trade beverages. Use of buying power is about being mindful, not judgmental. Champions of local food such as Alisa Smith and JB Mackinnon, who base their delightful book on a year's experience eating only *The 100 Mile Diet*, use their storyline as a conceit, hooking people into the drama of their challenge with an otherwise mundane set of chores. However, the real issue is embodied energy, not miles from farm to table. Transportation accounts for only 14 per cent of fossil fuels used in the food system. Nor is local food a diet, a word most people in the Global North automatically equate with food changes. Sustainable foods require a system overhaul, not a diet overhaul. And a good system design has to be balanced in terms of the many elements it works with, including the ability of food producers in distant lands to live more sustainably than they otherwise could. Fair trade can be a 'glocal' hybrid.

Duty of care

Kevin Morgan put down the newspaper article on Canada's runaway rates of diabetes, leaned across the breakfast table toward me, raised the furrow of his brow in that Welsh way, and whispered as if he was saying something seditious: 'Do you people not have a duty of care?'

I guess if careless driving, child neglect and professional misconduct are illegal, there must be a duty of care behind that, I said. But how does that relate to diabetes? Well, the duty of care is all the rage in Europe, where the ills of obesity account for 10 per cent of health costs. Morgan, an expert in government food purchasing at Cardiff University, told the conference we were both speaking at that the duty of care was helping create a 'new moral economy of food'.

Conventional government policy on food purchasing is determined by three factors, he says: cost, cost and cost. Allowable costs got so low that 'the kitchens and ovens went, and in came the scissors and microwaves' for opening and heating prefab food packages. Concern for health consequences led to accusations of being the would-be commissar of the nanny state.

'That accusation was the most spectacular innovation in the history of the food industry,' Morgan says. 'It had the same impact on [reform initiatives by] politicians as Kryptonite did on Superman.' But then came the duty of care, based on the notion that the government should protect its vulnerable citizens, especially children.

Morgan developed the idea of the 'double dividend' of school-meal programs. They can create benefits for student health and local jobs, he says. He was talking the language of Scotland's newly autonomous government, eager to launch a 'quality food revolution' that could overturn its record as the sick man of Europe. In 2002, before celebrity chef Jamie Oliver goaded the English government, the Scots released a health panel report called Hungry for Success. It favored a 'whole school approach' that encouraged nutritional eating, socializing during meals, farm visits, school gardens, cooking clubs, learning about food in class, and so on. Parents were involved too. So were school chefs, encouraged to experiment and reach for the stars with seafood risotto, spicy Cajun wraps and South African *bobotie*, a spiced meat and egg dish.

One school district in East Ayrshire, west of Glasgow, took the Hungry for Success ball and ran with it, piloting a Food for Life model promoted by the pro-organic Soil Association. In 2007, the Soil Association and its partners received almost £17 million pounds (more than $26 million) from the UK lottery fund to promote Food for Life across the UK. One feature of the program is the Food for Life Catering Award. Schools, universities and hospitals, even restaurants, achieve a bronze, silver or gold award by freshly preparing 75 per cent of meals served, purchasing sustainable fish and meat that satisfies UK animal-welfare standards, and adding organic, fair-trade, free-range and locally sourced foods to their menu, while promoting healthy eating.[11] An evaluation of the program's impact on schools published in 2011 indicates that students at the 3,800 participating schools are eating more vegetables and have improved test scores, while more than 'three pounds of social, economic and environmental value was created for every one pound spent on Food for Life menus, mostly in the form of new jobs in the local economy'.[12] This is grist to the mill of Morgan's theories of the new economy of disadvantaged areas, where 'civic capacity, public-private partnership and a political leadership which is honest and creative' step into the breach of do-nothing central governments and lead people out of the cheap food desert.

Putting food on the public plate

Meanwhile, across the Atlantic, another experiment in what Morgan calls 'putting food on the public plate' is taking hold at the University of Toronto. In September 2006, the lawn in front of the student council center was the launchpad for the University's program to introduce local and sustainably produced food to its 70,000 students – one of the largest student bodies of any university in North America, and therefore the largest local and sustainable food-purchasing program. The deal brings food from surrounding farmland to campus cafeterias, through the university's commitment to purchase an increasing percentage of its food from Ontario farmers who meet standards for environmental and social responsibility.

The new watchword for many is 'local and sustainable'. Get used to those two formerly distinct words rolling off the tongue together, with the same feel as macaroni and cheese, research and development, health and well-being, equity and diversity, peanut butter and jam. 'Local and sustainable' is the new kid on the food block, taking on the junk-food juggernaut of distant and unsustainable. Local Food Plus (LFP), which helped set the rules for the deal between the University of Toronto and food-service providers, certifies farmers and processors who actively seek local sales, while promoting animal and farm worker well-being, energy-efficient practices, pesticide reduction and working landscapes respectful of biodiversity. (The founder of Local Food Plus, Lori Stahlbrand, is my wife.) The chemical-use standards are less strict than organic, but the standards for social and environmental sustainability are higher. LFP's focus is on helping as many farmers as possible move towards more sustainable practices, working to avoid a problem when 'the perfect is the enemy of the very good'. As important as the certification is, the market-development program which links certified farmers and processors with institutional buyers, especially universities and municipalities, is as vital. Since its launch, the program has spread to Montreal's McGill University and several Ontario municipalities, as well as to restaurants and retailers.

It surprised me that a university would ever step up to the plate to use its purchasing power and prestige to put local and sustainable food on the map. But in a world of non-responsive institutions, post-secondary institutions stand out like a green thumb for being obliged to respond to students and faculty. Colleges and universities, often accounting for 10-20 per cent of local populations and economies, wield a lot of money and people power. Michael M'Gonigle and Justine Stark argue in *Planet U: Sustaining the World, Reinventing the University* that universities can and should use their purchasing power to set the standard for wages, building practices, waste management, and local, sustainable food in their communities.

In the US, meanwhile, college and university students are issuing the Real Food Challenge. The idea is to increase the procurement of 'real food' – defined as local/community-based, fair, ecologically sound and humane – to 20 per cent nationwide by 2020. Organizers of the campaign say this will mean shifting '$1 billion of annual college food purchases away from industrial agriculture towards local, sustainable, and fair sources'. Launched in 2008, the Real Food Challenge provides a way for students across the country to network and learn from each other as they develop campaigns on their own campuses, leveraging 'the power of youth and universities to create a healthy, fair and green food system'. The organization began as a program of The Food Project, a Boston, Massachusetts-based non-profit founded in the early 1990s. Real Food Challenge organizers offer a variety of supports to student food activists, including regional summits, leadership development opportunities, and a calculator to assess current campus purchases.

Urban agriculture

In a world that is half urban, urban agriculture simply makes sense. Food is only one product of an urban farm; other byproducts include environmental education, community development, resource and waste management, personal skill and esteem building, employment readiness training, fitness and nutrition. There are so many benefits and paybacks that every municipality can afford at least one animator on staff to help people organize and start gardens. In the following pages, I'll introduce three approaches that demonstrate how urban agriculture embodies what multifunctional agriculture is about.

Growing Power in the US

Retired basketball star Will Allen, founder of Growing Power, manages almost two dozen employees and more than a hundred volunteers who work in six greenhouses linked to a food retail outlet, commercial kitchen, livestock and beekeeping operation on the outskirts of Milwaukee, close to an Afro-American neighborhood Allen serves. Allen gave me a tour that showed off the scrap wood, volunteers and sheer grit behind Growing Power, which is about teaching kids from the nearby Afro-American neighborhood to 'keep coming back and not quit. The most powerful thing about this place is that people can come and see it, and leave ready to pick up a shovel and do it.'

The power source for the business is the second greenhouse, which houses compost. Every week, Allen gets 2,000 kilograms of mash from an organic brewery, 500 kilos of coffee grounds from local restaurants, and tons of fruit and vegetables that arrived at local food banks too late to be edible. This is Allen's money machine. Composting throws off enough heat to keep the greenhouses warm through Milwaukee's freezing winters. Huge bins are breeding grounds for tens of thousands of red wriggler worms that break down the food scraps and produce castings that go into compost teabags called Milwaukee Black Gold. A bin's worth of tea bags sell for $36,000. 'It would take a rancher 300 steers to equal the value of my worm livestock,' says Allen, a six-foot seven-inch gentle giant.

His other livestock dominate the fourth greenhouse, where a 16,600-liter container hosts 4,000 tilapia, small fish that do well in shallow and still water. For about eight months, the fish eat algae, water lettuce, duckweed and worms, all grown in the complex, before they reach their final weight, about two-thirds of a kilo, and are sold for meat. Allen turns that eight-month waiting period into a revenue stream by channeling tilapia excrement and compost tea to hydroponic trays that feed a wide range of herbs and greens, including watercress, cilantro, basil, eddo and baby bok choy. About 5,000 pots of herbs grow in the enriched water, ready to be shipped to local chefs who clip fresh sprigs of herbs just before they serve meals. Chefs lease their pot of herbs for $50 a month, and then return them for another.

The last greenhouse has raised beds where salad greens are planted thickly along hills of compost. The salad greens have their own pup tent to hold the heat from the ground and compost, so no other heat source is needed to get them through the winter. Outside the greenhouse are goats, rabbits, ducks, chickens and bees that produce 300 kilograms of honey from white clover in nearby fields.

Allen's hope is to show that a producer on one acre (0.4 hectares) of land, humming with 'closed loop' systems that convert 'waste' into a resource, can provide 1,000 people with healthy and affordable food basics. He estimates that once a system is ramped up, one person can make a decent income from one acre.

City farming in Sri Lanka

It's not very different in Sri Lanka or Uganda. 'It's all about the brown agenda,' says Luc Mougeot, as he bounds up a stairwell to a McGill University workshop with city farmers from Sri Lanka, Argentina and Uganda. Seeing my eyes glaze over, Mougeot explains that the brown agenda came out of the United Nations Agenda 21 of 1992. It's about redeeming and converting urban waste, such as dishwater, rainwater and food scraps, into a resource for food production. In an ideal scenario, the farmer would be paid twice, once for composting, and once for growing food.

At the workshop, Dr CD Palathiratne, the Chief Medical Officer of Colombo, Sri Lanka's largest city, spoke about people in the shantytowns, where 46 per cent of the population crowd onto 12 per cent of the land – 'squatting' near floodplains, garbage dumps, refineries or power lines. Access to running water, flush toilets, sewers or green space is rare. Palathiratne promotes city farming to provide income opportunities for women, low-cost nutrition for families, and herbal remedies in the Ayurvedic healing tradition. He encourages shantytown squatters to grow five plants rich in protein, minerals and vitamins – ginger and wild asparagus are the most recognizable to Westerners – that can creep up walls and fences, handle the cramped quarters of windowsills, or thrive in baskets hanging from roofs or containers resting on ledges. Some of the leaves are ground into porridge and cooked up as survival food to prevent malnutrition. Some leaves are bought by the city, processed in 20 city dispensaries into herbal medicines, and given free to the poor when they're sick, saving the medical system from paying for expensive imports of Western pharmaceuticals. Colombo's city planners follow the same 'hope-giving approach' to engage shantytown residents in 'community action planning', he says. They work with residents to compost waste water and 'humanure' (human excrement) for food production, thereby keeping them from contaminating water supplies, a major cause of illness in the Global South.

That's the combination Mougeot is looking for. 'I'm as interested in the inputs for urban agriculture as the outputs,' he says, a reference to the fact that city crops can be irrigated with wash water and fertilized with composted humanure, while city livestock can convert kitchen food scraps into protein as well as manure that produces biogas energy. Waste water, food scraps and humanure fit the definition of pollution as 'good resources in the wrong place', since the problem is not with them, but the fact that there's no place to put them to work in the farmless city. By keeping together the whole life-cycle of agriculture, 'urban agriculture is a way to make cities more efficient in the way they use resources', says Mougeot. This kind of agricultural multi-tasking deserves brownie points in a world that's more than half-urban.

Care farms in the Netherlands

All agriculture has the potential to be multifunctional and to address many social, cultural, health, economic and environmental goals. But urban agriculture has an extra list of multiple functions that cities in the Netherlands are the first to explore. Certain farms in and near the city are identified as 'Care farms' and paid a fee to provide some kind of care. In Almere, a biodynamic farm serves as an outdoor classroom for schoolchildren and provides work for people with mental disabilities. To the west of Amsterdam are care farms with a mandate to protect migrating birds in the course of farming.

Ten kilometers from the centre of Amsterdam sit a series of greenhouses stretching over three hectares – Landsijde Care Farm. Since 2009, professional horticulturalist and care farmer Jeroen Rijpkema has provided a hot meal, a team of therapists, and a job for about 80 people addicted to alcohol or drugs and without a place to call home. The fee paid by the city for this service covers about half his expenditures. From the city's point of view, the money is well spent because the people are in a warm, safe and healthy place, and are not on the street begging or getting in trouble with the law. Instead they have ongoing access to both professional counseling and work skills that could help them find their way to another life. The clients are paid 10 euros ($11) a day, and work at their own pace, quite a bit slower than on a commercial farm and with no complicated or dangerous tools or chemicals. The city gets its money's worth just by keeping people in a safe place, where they are out of harm's way and don't end up in very expensive places such as hospitals or courts.

The major crop is tomatoes. They grow in soil because the crews prefer working with soil, rather than in more mechanized hydroponic environments. Tomatoes have the advantage of being red and easy to identify, and the plants are trained to grow so most of the picking can be done at waist level, without a need to crouch or climb a ladder. The tomatoes are mostly sold at slightly above-market rates to two restaurants that agree to make purchases fulfilling their voluntary commitment to Corporate Social Responsibility. How much more civilized, healing or productive can food production get?

Alternative Land Use Services

Brian Gilvesy used to grow tobacco on his 140-hectare ranch in southwestern Ontario, but now works with Texas Longhorn cattle, endangered prairie grasses, wild birds, restored woodlands, and clean, cold creek water safe for wild fish. Some of his customers pay him a premium price for his drug-free, free-range, energy-conserving beef. And then he has other customers – or maybe they could be called stakeholders or partners – who pay him to grow back the endangered tall-grass prairie that provides habitat for birds hatching their young, to keep the creek that flows through his land clean and cool, to stabilize the fragile sandy soils that he says 'can turn into a beach in a heartbeat' by restoring 50 hectares of hardwood forest. Bringing this kaleidoscope of customers, stakeholders, partners and well-wishers together is Alternative Land Use Services or ALUS.

On a hay-wagon ride around his farm, I check out the three hectares of tall-grass prairie, which performs multiple functions. With roots that go five meters deep, the grass sucks down carbon from the air, which offsets global warming, stabilizes the sandy soil, and lets rainfall percolate slowly so it doesn't flashflood into the creek. It also provides nesting grounds for birds and even feed for the cattle. ALUS buys the prairie-grass seed, and pays Gilvesy to leave the field alone until mid-July, when the birds move on. The cattle are invited in for a feed, which Gilvesy says 'makes them fat and sassy', and ensures their beef is lean and well-priced. 'As I see it, society gets the use of my field for 10 months of the year, while I and my cattle only use it for two months,' he says, so it's fair that society pay its share of the overhead costs.

'We're where the water for this area is born,' Gilvesy says, so he works hard to keep it clean and cool, the way the fish need it to be, and the way the townsfolk like to have the water coming into their filtration plant. A variety of organizations, including the town water utility, give him a fee for his extra troubles to keep the creek clear and cool. ALUS also donates 30 bird boxes to house 60 bluebirds that eat flies off the back of the cattle, saving Gilvesy the cost of spraying pesticides on their backs, keeping their bodies and the nearby creek pesticide-free.

At this stage, ALUS can pay Canadian farmers between $30 and $450 per hectare, depending on how much time they spend on eco-service activity and the extent of eco-service they provide. A leading economic thinker in this field, Pablo Gutman, estimates that three trillion dollars a year could be profitably invested this way, paying low-income farmers around the world for non-food services that benefit the planet's soil, air, water, scenery and carbon storage.[13]

A terrible punster but a lot of fun on a hayride, Gilvesy attracts a lot of people to his farm tours, and often ends up selling some beef direct, bypassing the middleperson. His meat is also certified by a local environmental organization, which earns him a premium at local restaurants. 'We used to be the people with a problem. Now, we're in the solutions business,' the former tobacco farmer says. 'Farmers can grow back wildlife habitat just like they grow any other crop. That's the sweet spot. It's win-win-win all over the place. I can say to the public 'Now I work for you; just give me some support.'

Farms of the future will be classified as being in the service sector, not just the commodity sector. A good farm produces two kinds of services. There are environmental services such as clean air and water. And there are economic, health and social services, sometimes called 'distributed benefits', a term developed by energy gurus Amory Lovins and Paul Gipe. In other words, the social and economic benefits from local food production are often worth more to a local community than any money savings from cheaper long-distance food.

Consider job creation. Having farms in a community helps to create jobs in four ways. First, farms can create jobs making or repairing farm tools and buildings. Second, farms can create jobs – perhaps in an ice cream plant in a dairy district. Third, farms provide direct employment, maybe a summer job for a local student. Fourth, farmers create a 'multiplier effect' when they spend their earnings on a haircut or restaurant meal. Local food security is yet another distributed benefit, since local farms are a food lifeline in the event imports are blocked by an emergency. Add the heritage value of old family farms and farm tours for local schoolchildren studying food-related topics, and the list of distributed benefits keeps growing.[14]

If we can find ways to pay fair value for these services, farmers can earn a double dividend – a premium price paid by the customer for higher-quality food, and a fee from the public for all the services. A rancher like Gilvesy may get a good price for the rich taste and extra nutrients in grass-fed beef, for example, and then receive a second payment from agencies appreciating the enhanced water quality, and the new jobs in the tourism industry stimulated by scenic farm fields.

Seeds of hope

Eco-services have been the coming thing in farming since some 2,000 ecologists and scientific reviewers from 95 countries worked on the 2005 United Nations *Millennium Ecosystem Assessment Synthesis Report*. The UN report reviewed a range of otherwise-costly services that farms can produce economically: storing carbon in the soil (by planting deep-rooted grasses, for instance) to reduce global warming; pre-cleansing river water for the nearby town water utility; providing habitat for birds and small animals (with hedgerows, for instance); and preserving genetic diversity of plants and livestock that might prove invaluable in the event of disease outbreaks. Unlike conservation areas and national parks, all this can happen on working landscapes – that is, landscapes that are being actively farmed. Calculating the economic value of such services is relatively straightforward. If high-quality river water lowers city costs for water filtration by a million dollars a year, local farmers can profitably be paid a million dollars a year for on-farm measures protecting water quality – planting trees or deep-rooted grasses near waterways, reducing pesticides, keeping livestock out of the river, and so on.

The UN report costs out the value of services from a hectare of Canadian marsh – storage and cleansing of water run-off, habitat for birds, cooling of the nearby area, for example – at $4,000 a year. By contrast, the value of food produced on the same hectare is $2,100. In a cheap food system which only pays farmers for food, the farmer will fill in the marsh and grow food on it, make $2,100 a year, while the general public pays $4,000 for additional infrastructure to make up for the loss of marsh services. In a smart food system, the farmer will be paid $4,000 for services rendered by his physical plant, society benefits from $4,000 worth of services, and taxpayers avoid taxes to cover farm subsidies. This is what system planning encourages – maximizing the output of real food, not minimizing its price.

Few sectors can match food for distributed benefits. That's why it's such a false economy to organize a food system exclusively on the basis of sticker price. The corporate chains that enforce and deliver cheap food come up short when it comes to the chain reactions that create a vibrant local business community. The deregulated free-trade mania that has driven food policy since 1995 neglects half the economic potential of food and farming.

Farmer-scientists

In 2012, I toured peasant communities in Honduras as a guest of a farm organization called FIPAH, the Foundation for Participatory Research with Honduran Farmers, which partners with USC Canada, a development non-profit that I volunteer with. The idea for FIPAH came to Honduras via Sally Humphries, a scholar from Guelph, Ontario, who had learned about it in Colombia. Honduras is the original banana republic. It is characterized by both spectacular beauty and grinding poverty. The fertile valley area near the airport is dominated by plantations stretching as far as the eye can see, producing fruit and palm-oil biofuel for export. Two hours away by car, indigenous people, who once lived in the fertile area and turned it into one of the world's centers of origin for domesticated foods, now farm thin and poor soil on steep mountainsides, totally exposed to frequent hurricanes. They lost trace of their native language about a hundred years ago, of their native religion (though not spirituality), and there is no sign of traditional clothing. They are allowed their heritage of corn and beans. Before the project I am touring was started, people in mountain communities regularly ran out of food for six weeks during what they called 'the Junes'.

In 1998, FIPAH set up CIALs, local agricultural research committees, in several communities, some geographic and some geared to youth. There are now

Seeds of hope

85 CIALs with over a thousand members. Their project is to provide the kind of breeding and on-farm assistance to small farmers that the government provides to big farmers.

Marvin Gomez co-ordinates CIALs in the northern mountainous area we're visiting. The son of an indigenous activist, this university graduate in agronomy is short, lean and clean-cut, with a gentle smile. He and his CIAL members have worked wonders with seeds they've developed together. They have perfected two new varieties of corn, one called Santa Cruz and one an upgraded Capellin, which requires no fertilizers or pesticides. Each year's seeds are carefully chosen in the field, based on how well they withstood storms and produced big yields, then reviewed at home where they're selected on the basis of taste and nutrients. One CIAL member showed me fertilizing pebbles he found along the top of his mountain, which can be crushed and added to compost to provide 50 minerals. Gomez likes to say they have become farmer-scientists, though few of them finished elementary school. Over the life of the project, productivity has increased by 500 per cent. There are no more of 'the Junes', I'm told.

But these accomplishments are dwarfed by what has happened to people. On one of our mountaintop tours, we were joined by about 20 government officials. As we climbed up the mountains, women posted about every 75 meters explained how seeds were selected. The previous night, I had read myself to sleep with an article about the low self-esteem of women in these communities. Many were embarrassed to meet or speak to individuals they hadn't known all their lives, and had no sense they could ever do anything outside the home. Yet here they stood, ready to explain to government bureaucrats how plots are laid out scientifically so only the best seeds are picked. The same self-confidence holds in community affairs, where a typical woman now holds two or three volunteer positions. Female participation is a must on all CIAL executives. Men have changed too as they have gained more control over their lives. 'As a human being, I'm different,' one tells me. 'I used to use pesticides, and I used to drink. I've been sober for four years.' This community project is a vehicle for personal transformation. 'We're growing as people. We are learning lots of things,' a woman tells me. One young but extremely articulate teen tells me he is 'excited to learn. I feel hopeful because people are accompanying me in this challenge. We need to motivate ourselves to move forward.'

Though he is hired as an agriculture expert to guide the community search for improved seeds, Gomez recognizes food brings people together, but does not define all their interests. The CIAL teaches public speaking to build self-confidence, leadership and advocacy skills needed in the communities. It lobbies to bring senior-school grades to hillside hamlets so youth can gain an education without having to leave and so rural people win respect and pride as people worthy of education and leadership. It helps farmers raise cows, chickens, fruits and vegetables so they can have a varied and nutritious diet. It supports clean drinking water and toilets and more efficient, less smoky, wood stoves to promote public health and dignity of the person. It favors open fields where boys and girls can play soccer together and learn that rural life is also about having fun. It provides loans to help farmers develop artisanal products and become entrepreneurs. 'We are not just concerned with yield, but with food security and food sovereignty,' says Gomez.[15]

I was particularly drawn to Candida Cruz, who kept a brisk pace ahead of me for the 1.5-kilometer hike up the steep mountain slope of her family farm. She was kind enough to bring a horse along in case I needed to take a rest on the way up. 'Life here is hard but good,' she said, in response to my question about what advice she would give to young people. 'I feel great,' she said. 'It's not just men who can grow food. I don't like to depend on anyone. I like to depend on myself.' She oversees 3.6 hectares of land covered with beans and corn and walks about three kilometers a day to do it.

Candida is 72. Lacking spending money, she doesn't smoke or drink. She has to walk everywhere. She helped me refine an idea I developed with others on another trip to Mexico.[16] For two billion of the world's people making less than two dollars a day, for all intents and purposes surviving in a cashless economy, the next step forward they might choose could be 'subsistence-plus' – the comforts of good food, a home, close friends, open air, exercise, an unbelievable view, all the best things in life that come free, plus a little money to buy some extras – rather than take up the wild goose chase of more happiness in the city. That could be very trans-formative change for two billion people, and could eliminate extreme rural poverty and hunger.

For some reason, while I was in the mountains of Honduras, my mind drifted to a statement of the French existentialist philosopher Jean-Paul Sartre. 'Freedom is what you do with what has been done to you,' he said. Honduras is a stark reminder of all that has been done to so many people in the world. But it also offers a panoramic view of what people can do by working sensitively and mindfully with the food humans have co-evolved with over 200,000 years. We might just do this.

1 I Perfecto, 'Organic Farming Can Feed the World (Part 1), www.organicauthority.com/blog/?p=514 **2** J Vidal, 'India's rice revolution,' in J Madeley, ed, *Food for All: The Need for a New Agriculture*, Zed, 2002. **3** C Levkoe, 'Towards a transformative food politics,' *Local Environment*, 16,7, Aug 2011. **4** K Morgan, 'Feeding the City: The challenge of urban food planning,' *International Planning Studies*, 2009, 4 (4). **5** Thanks to GW Stevenson et al, 'Warrior, Builder, and Weaver Work: Strategies for Changing the Food System' in C Hinrichs, T Lyson, *Remaking the North American Food System*, University of Nebraska Press, 2007. **6** Longfield spoke to four of six orientations to policy reform identified in P Campsie, *Food Connects Us All: Sustainable Local Food in Southern Ontario* (Metcalf Foundation, 2008). **7** London Food Link, *Good Food for London 2012, How London boroughs can* secure a healthy and sustainable food future for everyone. **8** 'Organic Food Trends Profile', www.AgMRC.org **9** P Howard, 'Who owns Organic? From roots to suits.' *PCC Sound Consumer*, Jan 2007; V Cuddiford, 'When Organics Go Mainstream.' *Alternatives Journal*, Sep 2003; M Sligh and C Christman, *Who Owns Organic?* RAFI USA, 2003. **10** transfair.ca.en/fairtradetown; fairtrade.org.uk; tinyurl.com/c2ajaes **11** nin.tl/YUcolp **12** Good food for all: The impact of the Food for Life Partnership, accessed at tinyurl.com/bwfdrp4 **13** P Gultman, 'Ecosystem Services' in *Ecological Economics*, Vol 62, Nos 3-4, 2007, pp 383-387. **14** A Lovins, 'Small is Possible', Rocky Mountain Institute, Mar 2002; P Gipe, *Community Power, The Way Forward*, Canadian Renewable Energy Alliance, Aug 2006. **15** Sally Humphries et al, 'Linking Small Farmers to the Formal Research Sector', Algren network paper No 142, Jan 2005; Humphries et al, *Opening Cracks for the Transgression of Social Boundaries*, World Development, 2012. **16** The idea of 'subsistence-plus' was developed with Michael Sacco and Lori Stahlbrand.

Contacts and resources

Action Group on Erosion, Technology and Concentration
www.etcgroup.org

ALUS: Alternative Land Use Services
www.norfolkalus.com

American Community Gardening Association
communitygarden.org

Chocosol Traders
http://chocosoltraders.wordpress.com/

Community Food Centres Canada
www.cfccanada.ca

Fairtrade International
www.fairtrade.net

FIAN International
http://www.fian.org/

Food and Agriculture Organization of the United Nations
www.fao.org

Food First: Institute for Food and Development Policy
www.foodfirst.org

Food for Life Partnership
www.foodforlife.org.uk

Food Secure Canada
www.foodsecurecanada.org

FoodShare
www.foodshare.net

Growing Power, Inc
www.growingpower.org

International Federation of Organic Agriculture Movements
www.ifoam.org

Institute on Agricultural and Trade Policy
www. iatp.org

International Institute for Environment and Development
www. iied.org

La Via Campesina
viacampesina.org

Local Food Plus
www.localfoodplus.ca

Navdanya
www.navdanya.org

New Internationalist
newint.org

No-Nonsense Guide to World Food Facebook page
https://www.facebook.com/NoNonsenseGuidetoWorldFood

Oakland Institute
www.oaklandinstitute.org

Oxfam International
www.oxfam.org

Raj Patel
rajpatel.org

Real Food Challenge
www.realfoodchallenge.org

Slow Food International
www.slowfood.com

Sustain: The Alliance for Better
Food and Farming
www.sustainweb.org

Soil Association
www.soilassociation.org

Toronto Food Policy Council
tfpc.to

United Nations Special Rapporteur
on the Right to Food
www.srfood.org

USC Canada
usc-canada.org

WhyHunger
www.whyhunger.org

Index